Therapeutic Care for People with Intellectual Disabilities and Emotional Needs

Exploring a trauma-informed approach from professional and personal perspectives

Pat Frankish

Pavilion
PUBLISHING

Therapeutic Care for People with Intellectual Disabilities and Emotional Needs

Exploring a trauma-informed approach from professional and personal perspectives

Published by:
Pavilion Publishing and Media Ltd
Blue Sky Offices, 25 Cecil Pashley Way, Shoreham by Sea,
West Sussex, BN43 5FF

Tel: +44 (0)1273 434943
Email: info@pavpub.com
Web: www.pavpub.com

Published 2025

A catalogue record for this book is available from the British Library.

ISBN: 978-1-803884-30-1

Pavilion Publishing and Media is a leading publisher of books, training materials and digital content in mental health, social care and allied fields. Pavilion and its imprints offer must-have knowledge and innovative learning solutions underpinned by sound research and professional values.

Author: Pat Frankish
Copyeditor: Vivienne Button
Cover design: Emma Dawe, Pavilion Publishing and Media Ltd
Page layout and typesetting: Emma Dawe, Pavilion Publishing and Media Ltd
Printing: Independent Publishers Group (IPG)

Contents

Acknowledgements

I would like to acknowledge the many contributions to this volume. Without the many brave people who keep going as clients or staff we would not learn what we do. So many people have taught me so much over the last 40 plus years that I can only humbly say thank you. Let's hope that those who commission services can hear this message of trauma and hope.

Thank you to all of you who've contributed and those who read and use the knowledge we share.

Biographies

Nigel Beail is a Consultant Clinical Psychologist at South West Yorkshire Partnership NHS Trust and Professor of Psychology at the University of Sheffield. He has worked with people who have intellectual disabilities and autism for over 40 years. He has combined his clinical practice with research with a focus on psychotherapy and its outcomes for people who have Intellectual Disabilities. He has also promoted trauma-informed approaches in services for people who have intellectual disabilities. Nigel is past President of the European Association for Mental Health in Intellectual Disability, Past Chair of the British Psychological Society's Faculty for Intellectual Disabilities, and former Trustee of the British Institute for Leaning Disabilities. Nigel is a founder and Fellow of the Institute for Psychotherapy and Disability. He has published extensively on practice-based research from his clinical work.

Amanda Brock is the daughter of Dr Pat Frankish and works for Amara Care providing services for vulnerable people. Her life has always involved people with learning disabilities, with her first employment at a long-stay hospital when she was 18. She began working at Amara Care through several different employment opportunities, and also studied to gain more knowledge in the field of disability, and particularly those with a learning disability. Amanda has a Post Graduate Certificate in Management, Bachelor's in Science from the Open University and a Diploma in Health and Social Welfare. Within the business she has utilised all her management and working experience as well as undertaking Level 7 in Disability Psychotherapy.

Talitha Brock (RMHN) is a qualified nurse, having lived within an NHS family throughout her childhood. Since qualifying in 2001 at the age of 28, she has worked within older adult care, specifically dementia care, and has been employed in both health and social care setting, within NHS, private and third care sector organisations. This has included ward, day care, community care home and home care environments and supporting families of people living with dementia provided by 1:1 care, and/or peer support. She has strived to improve quality of life for families and advocate for those whose voice is not always heard. Positive dementia care and supporting people to use remaining skills and lead fulfilling lives to the best of a person, and families, ability is her ultimate goal.

Pat Frankish is a clinical psychologist and psychotherapist. She has spent her professional career developing the concepts of disability psychotherapy and emotional disability, with the hope that there will be more recognition of the emotional needs and the impact of trauma in early life for people who are intellectually disabled or traumatised. She has presented at national, European and wider international conferences since 1988, is a past president of the British Psychological Society and for the last 22 years has been a provider off supported-living services for people with complex needs. She continues to strive, through publications and training, to enable planners and service deliverers to understand the model of support and to recognise the possibilities for prevention of long term distress and the model for effective treatment.

Carol Hall is a mother of three grown-up children and has lived in her current town for the past 17 years. She was born in Aberdeen, Scotland and moved to England when her father relocated the family to work on a dairy farm in Lincolnshire when she was young. Her first job was working as a waitress in the restaurant where her mother worked and then moved on to other restaurants and became a manager. She then became a manager of an off licence and saw many different people with a lot of different issues in their lives. This was her first incline that she would like to help others if she could, so she became an IT tutor with her local authority, before taking a year out to enjoy spending more time with her family. She then applied for a Support Worker with Amara Care and has been with the company for almost 12 years.

Dr Paula Levett is a Principal Clinical Psychologist currently working in Devon & Torbay for an NHS service for children with a learning disability. She has also worked in a number of children's services in the Greater Glasgow area, including an LD-CAMHs service and as part of a small team who developed an LD-CAMHs service in Tameside. Dr Levett studied at the University of Glasgow to obtained D.Clin.Psy in 2003. She has been interested in the work of Dr Pat Frankish and the Disability Psychotherapy approach for around 15 years, and has introduced the FAIT approach to colleagues, special schools and families to increase awareness of the importance of understanding the emotional world and emotional development of children with learning disability.

Dr Erica McInnis is a Chartered and Consultant Clinical Psychologist and trained Disability Psychotherapist based in Manchester. Of Jamaican parentage, she has over 20 years' experience working across NHS, university, and community settings. During her NHS career, she specialised in enhancing the emotional lives of people with learning disabilities through a range of evidence-based approaches. She is the founder of Nubia Wellness and Healing CIC, where she delivers African-centred healing through workshops, therapeutic groups, and culturally grounded resources. She developed wellness products designed to put African Psychology into everyday practice. Dr McInnis has lectured on clinical and counselling psychology doctorate programmes and supervised doctoral research projects. She has published in peer-reviewed journals on disability psychotherapy and applies this perspective in clinical work, and has presented at European and international conferences, contributed to British Psychological Society (BPS) supervision guidance, and served on BPS committees influencing the profession.

David O'Driscoll is a psychoanalytic psychotherapist (UKCP) and historian specialising in trauma, loss, disability, and bereavement for Hertfordshire Partnership University NHS Foundation Trust, and a visiting lecturer at the Centre for Learning Disability Research at Hertfordshire University. His work involves individual and group work with service users and training and consultancy for staff teams. Prior to working in the NHS, David was a social worker. He was formally a director of Respond for five years and contributed two chapters to the Respond book exploring psychoanalytic psychotherapy, history and trauma. David is currently a council member of the Association for Psychoanalytic Psychotherapy in the Public Sector and the coordinator of its learning disability section. He is also Chair and a founder member of the Institute for Psychotherapy and Disability (IPD).

Valerie Sinason PhD is a widely published poet, writer, child and (now retired) adolescent psychotherapist and adult psychoanalyst. She has specialised in trauma and disability for 40 years and lectures nationally and internationally. Founder and now Patron for the Clinic for Dissociative Studies UK as well as President of the Institute for Psychotherapy and Disability, she was also on the Board of the ISSTD and received their 2017 Lifetime Achievement Award. She was given the British Psychoanalytic Council Innovation Excellence Award in 2022. Having worked at the Tavistock Clinic and St George's, she was also an Honorary Consultant Psychotherapist at the Cape Town Child Guidance Clinic and Acting Chair of the Bushman Heritage Centre New Bethesda.

Carrie-Anne Smith is 19 years old in a 40-something year old body and has Complex Dissociative Identity Disorder and Complex Post Traumatic Stress Disorder. They are system host and a survivor of Satanist Ritual Abuse. The system of which she is host are now working as an activities coordinator for Amara Care with people with learning disabilities, their first job in many years and surviving despite the daily challenges that arise due to the DID and abuse. Life went from being an existence to a life when Amara Care came into it. The system now says 'if it wasn't for Pat and Amanda we would not have survived and would have been most likely in the hands of the coven or worse.' In line with Amara Care's 'Creating Meaningful lives' motto, Carrie-Anne and all really are now living a meaningful life.

Foreword

by David O'Driscoll, *Chair of the Institute of Psychotherapy and Disability*

I am delighted to have been invited to write the foreword for this book. I first encountered Pat Frankish over 25 years ago, beginning my psychodynamic psychotherapy training. At that moment, the literature on working psychotherapeutically with this group was slim, so I was intrigued to discover her paper (Frankish, 1989), which alerted me to someone challenging the (then) conventional wisdom that psychotherapy was not possible with this population (O'Driscoll, 2009). This has been a feature of Pat's lifetime of work: the importance of speaking out and challenging the conventions of considered norms.

In my psychotherapy training, I did not receive any input on working therapeutically with this group, which is sadly still the case today (O'Driscoll, 2025). It was important to read about the work of like-minded clinicians and today we would place this paper at the start of 'disability psychotherapy'. I was also intrigued to read how she used the theories of Margaret Mahler: someone looking outside the conventional psychodynamic theories to understand this population, who was not so widely known. Mahler has become a key figure in the development of her FAIT model.

After finishing my training and obtaining a NHS psychotherapy position in 1999, I was soon puzzled by the lack of reference to trauma in most of my referrals, despite it being a key factor in their presentation. I soon realised this was because many colleagues did not fully understand the role of early trauma. Pat also explains that it is too painful for many of us to face trauma in the lives of people with people with learning disabilities. She highlights the role of 'primary trauma', which is vital in developing self and the ability to relate to others. This happens in early life before the person has developed a sense of self, known as 'individuation'. The Frankish model highlights the importance for a significant other or an attachment figure in the development of this. This is, in my opinion, another important insight that is still not fully understood today within services and I hope this contribution will enable colleagues to start addressing it, particularly as there is, today, such an emphasis on trauma-informed care.

Pat's other contribution is to acknowledge that while individual psychotherapy is important, it can only go so far. If we are serious about supporting meaningful lives, we must find ways to work with the support network. And sometimes this can be challenging, as I still experience in my work today, often support services still use the term, "attention seeking." Pat has emphasised the importance of training support staff, particularly in understanding emotional development and the impact of trauma. This is behind her model of Amara Care.

In this book Pat has gathered an impressive list of contributors, including my Institute of Psychotherapy and Disability colleagues Nigel Beail and Valerie Sinason. In the book there are also chapters on knife crime, dementia, and children's services. It is always good to hear the voices of service users, but I think it is particularly noteworthy to hear the experiences of support staff, who are rarely heard in publications like this. The value of this book is that it is written in a way that will make sense to anyone working with people with intellectual disabilities in all settings. I know it will be well received by this wider community.

References

Frankish, P. (1989) Meeting the emotional needs of handicapped people: A Psychodynamic approach. *Journal of Mental Deficiency Research*. **33**: 407-14.

O'Driscoll, D. (2009) 'A short history of psychodynamic psychotherapy for people with learning disabilities' in *Advances in Mental Health and Learning Disabilities*, Vol. 3 No. 4, pp.4-9, doi: 10.1108/17530180200900032.

O'Driscoll, D (2026) 'Implications for training: how the principles of Disability Psychotherapy can be integrated into mainstream psychotherapy training' in Sinason, V. and Vaga, A. (2025) *Disability Psychotherapy. What it is and why it is important*. (London: Routledge).

Preface

We are reaching a stage in society and in service provision where there is more recognition of the existence of trauma in people's lives. This is particularly true for people with intellectual disabilities, which is the main thrust of the contributions to this volume. However, there is also significant relevance for other groups, and the needs of those other groups are considered in some of the chapters. Notably, there is a substantial chapter on dementia, another about a young woman with physical disabilities, and another written by someone with Dissociative Identity Disorder (DID) – all with a fundamental acceptance of the impact of trauma in early childhood.

There have been several publications recently that began to explore in more detail the need for attachment-based support for people who have experienced trauma. The power of relationships is gradually being recognised and this is a significant breakthrough. Some of the chapter contributors have had, like myself, experience of the old long-stay hospitals – i.e., the institutions. That sort of care was quite de-personalising and attachments were, in fact, discouraged. It does seem to be taking a long time to work against those traditions.

Alan Skelly and Victoria Shimmens' 2024 book, *Love, Attachment and Intellectual Disability*, covers the issues in question and is a significant step forward. Their call for a fundamental shift in policy is very much supported by the contents of this volume. It feels like a long haul, from my first publication in 1989 to where we are now, but I am reassured by the fact that we have more people saying similar things – and more recognition of the emotional needs of people with disabilities, particularly intellectual disabilities.

If we go back to the beginning of thinking about the development of self, we probably need to look at the work of Sigmund Freud and Jean Piaget. Although their ideas are becoming more ingrained in modern practice, there is very little attention paid to what they said. Services have become more practical and less theoretical. This is probably prompted by a shortage of sufficiently trained personnel and by a shift in what is expected of professionals and families. Many aspects of modern life put families under pressure. It is now common practice for mothers and fathers to work, relying on secondary care for young children. This does not have to be harmful, so long as the secondary care applies the right principles and the handover is managed appropriately.

The very young child needs to know who their significant other safe person is at all times. When at home, they are very clear that it is one or both parents. When in secondary care, there needs to be a managed transfer of attachment figure from parent to support staff. This must be a named member of the support staff, rather than a general acceptance of the collective. Applying this simple rule all the time makes a significant difference to the emotional well-being of the child.

In this volume, we look at the development of services provided by my group of companies, together with an exploration of the difficulties encountered as a result of conflicting legislation. There is plainly a need for a new Mental Health Act and for more joined-up thinking in social care and housing, as well as better connectiveness between health and social care. Issues are discussed in the context of real-life stories.

Lessons from key practitioners

Then there are chapters from key people in the field of trauma-informed care, with Valerie Sinason and Nigel Beail sharing their journey with us. They follow a similar timeline to my own and both have history with the old long-stay hospitals. They, also like me, worked out some years ago that people with intellectual disabilities still have a rich emotional life, which is accessible to therapeutic care. I will be forever grateful to these two for the support they have given me over the years, for the sharing that has been possible. We have all been active within our professional organisations in this country, within European initiatives, and on a wider basis, including Valerie's activity in South Africa. These stories make for interesting reading, with a strong emotional content that continually reminds us of the basic humanity that we are all hoping to address.

We then go on to look at the report from Paula Levett, who has taken the Frankish Assessment of the Impact of Trauma in Intellectual Disability (FAIT) on board enthusiastically, putting it into practice across the whole children's service in Devon. It is encouraging to read about how effective this has been and it gives us a model for us to follow. The energy and enthusiasm that Paula has put into the model is fantastic. She has contributed markedly to the skill acquisition of her team, as well as other teams within her geographical area. It is a joy to read about what they have achieved for the young people whom they support. We can only hope that the adult services in that area carry the message forwards into the future services that the young people will need.

An intersectional perspective on trauma

Erica McInnis gives us another angle in understanding the trauma experienced by people on the basis of race and colour. This is a very moving chapter and highlights some of the things that have been in the news recently about young black men being disengaged – yet a further example of the impact of trauma and the need for trauma-informed services if we are to avoid more disasters. Erica is capturing cultural issues that exist within our country and our services and, in particular, services for young people. If people feel ostracised within society, they will potentially be traumatised. If we are not careful, we will end up with generations of traumatised people parenting the next generation of traumatised children, and so on.

People are moving around the world all the time and there is no such thing as a fixed population anymore. We need to be more tolerant of the differences between our cultures and be alert to the situations that leads to a traumatic response. If we consider young people who have issues stemming from race and colour, in addition to an intellectual disability, and have perhaps escaped from a war-torn country in order to seek refuge here in the UK, we can see why they may be traumatised. That is the first step towards beginning to address the trauma therapeutically.

Impact of trauma on people with other disabilities

I have included chapters about other client groups as well as people with intellectual disabilities. It has become very evident to me over the past few years that the progression of dementia is the emotional developmental model in reverse, and that people progressing through those stages can and should benefit from the emotionally nurturing environment that is advocated for people with intellectual disabilities and children more generally. I have been closely involved in the services that Tilly talks about and have seen the benefit that some distressed people with dementia have gained from having a therapeutic environment that provides them with the emotional security that they need. It would be good if all residential and nursing home facilities for people with dementia were able to recognise the stage that these people have reached and could provide the emotional environment that is required. It can be emotionally challenging for carers (whether family or paid carers), which is why it is necessary to provide support for the people doing the caring and recognise that they too can be traumatised by the shock of seeing the changes in their loved ones.

Susan's story gives us some insight into living with severe physical disabilities. I had tremendous respect for her determination during her lifetime. Susan was very strong-willed and was determined that she was not going to be treated as a second-class citizen. However, she had not had the opportunity to progress emotionally to a full state of individuation and therefore felt the need to punish people when they got things wrong. Susan had a point to make, which was an expression of her anger about her disability and her inability to live the life she would have chosen.

I have come across this situation many times with people who have cerebral palsy without a learning disability. It's almost as though having the knowledge of what could have been adds further punishment. It has become clear to me, in some families where a child has cerebral palsy, that there is confusion about intellectual ability in the presence of such physical disability. I remember, in particular, a young woman I knew who had a talking machine that she could use to say what she wanted. This was before iPads and readily available talking machines. What I found was that people would switch off her machine so that she could not express her wishes. This was, I think, a working-through of unresolved anger and disappointment on both sides.

There is no doubt that, as human beings, we are complex – and minds can be a blessing or otherwise! What we do need to accept is that we cannot possibly know everything that is going on for the people we are trying to support. We cannot even know for certain what is going on in our own heads a lot of the time, because we all have some unresolved issues from our own life experiences. What we *can* do is start with a blank sheet and try and work out what we can do to make life as anxiety-free as possible.

Carrie Anne's chapter suggests a way of helping people with DID to live a productive life. DID is one of the most complex conditions that we will ever come across. Living with lots of alternative identities within your own mind cannot be easy. Carrie Anne is able to chart, in her story, her escape from an abusive situation and her transition into a meaningful life. This could not have happened without the support of her funding organisation. Sadly, that funding has not been continued at the level that is truly required, but Carrie Anne made huge strides in spite of that. DID is probably one of the least-understood conditions and Carrie Anne does point you towards some other reading.

The value of speaking out

Perhaps the most moving part of the whole volume can be found in the real-life stories of individuals. Those who could consent have their names included; others have their name changed to protect their identity. All the people included in this volume were seriously traumatised in their early lives and have benefited noticeably from the therapeutic approach. It is not our intention to cause you distress in your reading, but more to enable you to take the ideas and the knowledge on board in your own services.

You do need to be brave enough to speak up at meetings, especially multidisciplinary team meetings where there may be very fixed views about behaviour or medication and such like. Regrettably, it does seem to be the case that the more complex people bring out – possibly through projection and introjection – some very negative feelings from the people who are meant to be supporting them. I have sat through many a multidisciplinary team meeting feeling as though I'm the only one talking sense!

I am aware that we all need to protect our own psyche, but we must be brave enough to speak out for the vulnerable people who cannot speak for themselves. When we realise that some people have been treated wrongly for 20 or 30 years (and sometimes longer), we can see why they are so emotionally cut off from people around them. They're often so distressed and despairing that they no longer expect anyone to help. Engaging them in a positive way forward can take time and patience but is nothing less than they deserve.

A model of care decades in the making

Much of what is in this work concerns the development of Amara Care, including the difficulties as well as the successes. It is a model of providing trauma-informed care that could be replicated across the country and further afield. We have been in the position to provide the model in a US state – and think it has been taken on board – but have received no recent communication from the organisation in question. One of their therapists attended our online training and was very enthusiastic about delivering the model to their whole service. Paula's chapter demonstrates that it can be delivered to a whole service and this is clearly what we would like to see. The online training and the Community of Practice make it very easy for people to engage with the process of establishing the model within their services.

The motivation for me, throughout this work, has been to try to provide a simple approach to a complex problem. If we consider that psychoanalysts would want to see their patients five times a week for an hour session each day in order to process their initial trauma, we realise that this is not going to be possible for the majority of the population. What the FAIT and the trauma-informed care model provide is a way of capturing the impact of early trauma to inform a care plan that can work and relieve the pain and distress that the person is experiencing.

Looking to the future

Traditionally, people with intellectual disabilities (and sometimes other disabilities) would be excluded from therapeutic services. There is perhaps some sort of elitism attached to intelligence, but this does not seem to be appropriate in the 21st century. It may, of course, be the complete opposite – i.e., people do not feel adequate to work with people who are obviously complex. We have learned a lot during the past 40 years in this particular field and hope that what we have learned will be put into practice across most services within the next few years.

I reflect on the impact of various pieces of legislation in my lifetime, especially the Mental Health Act and the Education Acts, which led to changes in the categorisation of people and resulted in the availability of more appropriate services. There is a need to go much further now that we know more about what is possible and it is hoped that this collection of stories will facilitate more development on this front.

I hope you will all feel that you can identify with the contents of this volume and be prepared to join the movement towards recognition of emotional disability as a diagnosis (or condition) and as a trigger for appropriate intervention.

References

Skelly, A., and Shimmens, V. (2024) *Love, Attachment and Intellectual Disability.* Shoreham: Pavilion Publishing.

Introducing the model of care

Chapter 1: Introduction

The general recognition of the impact of trauma probably goes back to the impact on men serving in wars and coming back with very serious Post-Traumatic Stress Disorder (PTSD), known then as 'shell-shock'. However, the impact of trauma on people with intellectual disabilities has only been recognised relatively recently. The impact of attachment issues on children has been recognised for some years but, again, children with intellectual disabilities were largely excluded from consideration.

One of the pictures that comes to mind for me whenever I think about this is the child with a disability who cannot run after their mother and therefore is left downstairs while she goes upstairs to clean the bedrooms and make the beds. We would not leave a two-year-old alone downstairs if they were capable of creating havoc or hurting themselves. But if your child cannot do that they are more likely to be left, even though – as a disabled child – they are probably even more traumatised than a non-disabled child by losing sight of their attachment figure.

Recognition of the impact of trauma on the mental health of the general population has become more widespread in recent years and this has gradually expanded to include the impact on those with an intellectual disability. What has happened, though, is that most of the work has looked into people traumatised by events that have usually occurred after the person has established a sense of self. In order to develop a strong sense of self, it is vital that the person has available to them a 'significant other' attachment figure – by this we mean a person who keeps them and their world safe, usually a parental figure. In the absence of that basic human need, there tends to be what I would call 'primary trauma', which interferes with the development of self and the ability to relate to other people.

John Bowlby identified these problems and wrote extensively about the need to maintain attachments for healthy development of the personality. We would look back on it now as common sense, but it was not at the time of Bowlby's writing, and many people still have difficulty accepting the idea that trauma can occur before children reach the age of three or four. It has become evident to me in my years of clinical work that the most distressed people I meet are those who are functioning emotionally as toddlers.

We then have to question why that is the case. Why do people with intellectual and emotional disabilities seem to miss out on an appropriate diagnosis and intervention? It seems to me that the issue is perhaps too painful for many of us to recognise and accept. It seems unlikely that people would deliberately traumatise their disabled infant but, at the same time, we know that services are often not adequate to support struggling parents. Parents have the usual stresses of looking after a new baby and young child, along with adjusting to the extra needs of a disabled child. It is also a fact that some disabilities do not become obvious immediately. I think of the child who sleeps a lot, with parents who think how fortunate they are to have a baby who does not keep them up all night, without realising that a disability is the reason their child is not awake. This can lead to anxiety and stress in the parents – who need support, not criticism – which can then traumatise the child further as a result.

How intellectual disability has been written about in the past

There are a number of publications now that capture the development of thinking in the field of intellectual disability. It is something that has interested me for many years and led me to write the book *Disability Psychotherapy*, which was published in 2016. I would like to think that it has had some impact on the design and delivery of services for people with intellectual disabilities. However, I do find that there remains almost a resistance to recognising early trauma. Most services who would describe themselves as trauma-informed care are still offering interventions that fail to grasp the primacy of the trauma. Having worked with a lot of staff providing trauma-informed services and carried out a lot of training of staff in my own services, as well as in schools, infant mental health services, and a range of health services, I have come to understand that the study of such primary trauma is painful and activates past trauma in those who are listening.

In *Disability Psychotherapy* (2016), I extensively consider the work of John Bowlby, Donald Winnicott and Margaret Mahler. They were all working in the second half of the 20th century and were saying things that really needed to be said and heard. With the development of community care, there has been a significant increase in the person-centred approach to support for people with intellectual disabilities. There has, at the same time, been a very strong movement for the use of positive behaviour support. This is a very active and positive way of offering support to people with intellectual disabilities. When Gary LaVigna and Thomas Willis first advocated the use of positive programming in the 1980s, it was taken on board with enthusiasm and has changed the lives of lots of people who were deemed to be unable to learn to behave differently.

Unfortunately, people with very early trauma are not necessarily able to respond to a positive approach. They are usually so cut off emotionally that they cannot value what is being provided for them if it expects them to respond and give something back. They have nothing to give back, so can only respond to interventions that give and give until they notice that they are being given to. This can take months, or sometimes years, but the investment makes a significant difference to the rest of their lives. Positive behaviour support is very effective in the right place at the right time.

The next significant publication was *Trauma and Intellectual Disability* (2021), a collection of chapters by a variety of people and edited by Nigel Beail, Alan Skelly and myself. In this book, we get lots of examples of work with trauma and different models of therapy that are effective in recognition of the emotional needs. This includes a chapter by an 'Expert by Experience', Roger Wilszwk, featuring a painful but positive story of his experiences. He cries out for people to listen and to hear. It's a powerful message to all of us. He stresses the need to help these children. If we can notice and intervene early with the right support, we could prevent so much distress.

In this volume, Dr Valerie Sinason – very eloquently – takes us through the history of disability, explaining that it is also a history of trauma. Valerie has been an ambassador for the models of trauma-informed care for many years and we owe an awful lot to her courage and determination to be heard. She has been an inspiration to me throughout my career. We have shared a number of conference presentations and have worked consistently to improve services for the traumatised people that we meet in our professional roles. As we both face retirement, we have attempted to make sure that what we have learned is committed to print for the use of others who follow.

Allan Skelly and I have both come up with assessments that can be used by other people. It is hoped that more people will use these assessments, learn from them, and continue to develop them further. There is no doubt in my mind that what we are finding in children and adults with intellectual disabilities will also be found in people without an intellectual disability but who have an emotional disability. It has become obvious to me, and I hope to others, that – although early trauma is more common in people with intellectual disabilities – it does happen to other people, especially young children with erratic family situations.

There does not seem to be enough support for young parents, leaving them to manage without necessarily knowing what to do. Healthy attachment is a primary requirement for all young people and, unfortunately, this is not necessarily understood by everyone with a new baby. New babies are very demanding and it's not easy, especially if you do not have a support network around you. Babies taken into care have to adjust their attachments – perhaps to several people – and recognition of the emotional trauma that this may cause is vital.

All support staff in children's services need to understand early trauma, look out for the signs, and be able to give the necessary advice and support to facilitate attachment. The FAIT assessment is very simple and quick to use and is appropriate to use with children under five, as well as all ages with a disability. Allan's assessment is equally relevant to children as well as adults. He stresses the need to recognise the impact of trauma on people who are in receipt of mental health services. There are so many people presenting with mental health difficulties at the present time who would clearly be assessed as having an emotional disability if such an assessment was available to them.

Emotional disability is a term that needs to come into much wider use. It is a term we have adopted to indicate people who have not progressed to individuation, a sense of self as separate from others. Ideally this happens about the age of 3 or 4 years old but may not if there is trauma. Children with intellectual disabilities are probably more at risk of early trauma because of issues of separation. It is expected that further research in the future will find a similar pattern for some mental heath conditions. The FAIT measures the stage of emotional development achieved and can therefore give pointers to when the trauma occurred.

Brett Kahr takes us into the forensic field and Biza Stenfert Kroese explores the cognitive approach in the same publication. Altogether, *Trauma and Intellectual Disability* has set out the history and what needs to be done. It has been followed by Victoria Shimmens and Allan Skelly's *Love, Attachment, and Intellectual Disability* (2024) – a significant piece of work in spelling out the need for love and attachment. Traditionally, services for people who are different in some way (for example, intellectual disability or mental health difficulties) have attempted to avoid any showing of true emotion. In the old days of institutions, staff were instructed specifically not to become attached to the people they were caring for and were frequently moved to another ward if it was detected that they were showing some signs of attachment.

We now know that this was cruel and attempt to make sure that it no longer happens. But we also know that anyone being cared for in an inpatient setting will have to tolerate contact from a lot of different staff, which makes it difficult for relationships to form. There must be a better approach, which really leads to much of what is in the following text about what can happen within community services. Victoria and Alan have produced some very poignant stories of real people (identities disguised) who have suffered from developmental trauma but have found a way forward by being provided with love and attachment. The right approach has allowed them to develop their sense of self and to grow into their best selves.

In my recent publication, *Understanding the Impact of Trauma* (2021), I have attempted to expand the theme to deepen our understanding – in particular, by including a number of case studies of people who have benefited from having their trauma understood and been provided with appropriate support and interventions. The publication you are reading now expands on that theme and includes significant reference to the difficulties that we encounter when we try to provide services for traumatised people within a traumatised system. It is sadly the case that there are never enough available interventions or enough primary assessments to identify the need for intervention. There is no doubt that early intervention would alleviate the strain on – and the cost of support for – traumatised adults and it is hoped that progress will be made in this direction.

Spreading the word

As we continue to develop ideas and knowledge about emotional disability (with its associated attachment issues), we come to the realisation that everybody needs to know. By everybody, I mean everybody involved in the delivery of services at all levels, especially those in day-to-day contact with the people in need. But it is equally, if not more, significant that those in charge of developing and commissioning services should understand what is actually required. There are a number of stories in this publication that highlight the difficulty of balancing housing needs, support needs, work and activity, as well as therapy. It does seem to be a miracle sometimes if all of these things are in tune and the individual is able to receive what they need.

There has been some progress during recent years but, when I reflect on my 40 years of active involvement as a clinical psychologist in services for people with intellectual disabilities, I am disappointed that there is not more accepted policy and leadership from the top. There is so much to be gained in preventing serious disturbance in adulthood if the issues are addressed in childhood. But I am an optimist and continue to write in the hope that more people read and respond. I know that my colleagues in this field – some of whom have contributed to this volume, and others whom I have referenced earlier – will continue the work after I need to retire.

References

Frankish, P. (2016) *Disability Psychotherapy: An Innovative Approach to Trauma-Informed Care*. London: Routledge.

Frankish, P. (2024) *Understanding the Impact of Trauma*. Shoreham: Pavilion Publishing.

Shimmens, V. and Skelly, A. (2024) *Love, Attachment, and Intellectual Disability*. Shoreham: Pavilion Publishing.

Beail, N., Frankish, P. and Skelly, A. (2021) Trauma and Intellectual Disability: Acknowledgement, Identification and Intervention. Shoreham: Pavilion Publishing.

Chapter 2:

Being Scientific with Unconscious Material – the Disability Psychotherapy Story

Going back to my early days as a psychology trainee, I recall the journey from my own conscious self to my unconscious self. What a journey! We spend most of our lives in the conscious mode and only seek the unconscious when things go wrong – or when we are learning.

I was more of a 'techie' in those days, having spent a lot of time developing a talking machine for a young girl with cerebral palsy. I don't think I had even considered the unconscious mind until I was given the opportunity to study at Liverpool University on a clinical psychology course. There was (and I hope still is) a very active psychotherapy group – the aim of which was to teach, guide and support those of us who were interested in exploring our own unconscious self and the way of working with others. This was in addition to our clinical psychology curriculum, requiring a further investment of time, energy, and personal commitment. I certainly never regretted the extra time that I gave to this element of my learning.

One of the plusses of this time at Liverpool University was the opportunity to work therapeutically with a young child with a learning disability. He was very distressed and in a care home with staff. He was almost unmanageable and causing great distress to the other children as well as the staff. I was asked to try therapy with him and, upon my agreement, a bare room (to avoid damage), a relevant box of toys, and ten sessions were all put in place. We were all apprehensive but he responded dramatically.

As soon as we were alone in the room with the toys, he visibly relaxed and showed me – through his play – what had happened to him. He didn't speak, so it was all acted out. It was very painful to witness his story of abuse and pain. He responded well to my interpretations of what he was showing me and he was able to make positive physical contact. After only one session, he was more relaxed with staff; after five sessions, he was mixing with the other children and showing interest in being toilet-trained. He taught me a lot and I took that learning into my future work.

Early influences

I was introduced to Sigmund Freud, Melanie Klein, Carl Jung, and others. I became fascinated and also much more aware of my own experience of trauma and how it shaped my life and my openness to the approach. Around this time, David Malan published his seminal text *Psychodynamic Psychotherapy and the Science of Psychodynamics* (1979), which was mind-blowing. It was a real and helpful attempt to make complex ideas more available to all. Elsewhere in this book, Nigel Beail talks about the application of Malan's work to therapy for people with learning disabilities. I was able to use Malan's model with my first client with Borderline Personality Disorder (now called Emotionally Unstable Personality Disorder (EUPD)).

I reflect now on the psychoanalysts who first had an impact on me, as that helps to describe the journey to where I am now. My first response to Freud was probably fairly typical in that I thought he had missed, and not understood, what was really happening to the young women he was seeing. This made me angry but also helped me in my journey towards feminism and 'woman power'. Over the years, we have come to understand that Freud was a man of his time.

I think we will always be grateful for the work that he put in to make sure that people began to listen and to try to understand what was happening with unconscious processes. Even the simple model of the id, the ego, and the superego was revolutionary at the time, and has been significant in contributing to our understanding of how human behaviour is driven by unconscious processes. This was the point at which we began to recognise the difference between the cognitive self and the emotional self. It is relatively recent that there has been some recognition and use of the term emotional disability, a core element of this volume.

Next was Melanie Klein, whom I found difficult to read and limited in that her study was of her own children, but her description of the 'depressive position' (ie, the experience of the self as wrong and others as punitive) impacted on me and has continued to do so. Seeing the process of a young child progressing from an omnipotent infant who ruled the world to a person able to balance good and bad in the same person was a significant step in my learning. It also helped me on my journey towards trusting observation. We do not have the luxury of the 24-hour intense observation that Klein had but we can begin to think along the same lines.

The way Klein spoke/wrote about love, guilt and reparation (the title of one of her books) and envy and gratitude (another of her book titles) just explained so much of the distress I was witnessing in my own therapy clients. It also helped me in my own self-analysis. I notice now when people have not achieved the resolution of the depressive position. But, as it is a hard concept to grasp, it is easier to use the terminology of rapprochement, with its behavioural presentation and description.

Klein was fairly closely followed, in my studies, by Michael Balint's *The Basic Fault* (1968). This took me into the area of very primary issues and helped even more to build up my picture of the impact of trauma in the very early years. I doubt that Balint is read extensively by most mental health professionals, but the idea that we can be impacted by very early life events is so important. So many people believe that we do not remember, or know, anything much about what happened before we could speak. This is clearly not right and, over the years, people have increasingly felt able to say so and to publish their work. If we have the basic fault from our primary relationship, it will impact on us for life and will affect the way we relate to others – although it can be addressed in deep therapy. I will go on to look at how it can be accommodated as we progress through the chapter.

Another influential figure was Eric Berne, for his work on transactional analysis (TA). This is the idea that we switch from child to adult to parent mode, depending on our own state of mind and the emotional environment we find ourselves in. By way of example, if we are hurt, we can drop into child mode quite easily; if someone else is hurt, we can assume the role of parent in response. In healthy relationships, we both stay in adult most of the time. Becoming more aware of what we do unconsciously allows us to bring more things into conscious control and develop our interpersonal skills.

TA skills are very useful in services where staff and clients need to relate to each other. Being aware of who is where and at any one time can facilitate healthy exchanges. Finding staff behaving in child mode is an indicator that they are struggling or one of the people they support needs to play. Finding staff being too parental can be unhelpful or sometimes needed. Finding all in adult mode is a relief! Managers need to be in adult mode most of the time. Of course, if all are successfully functioning in adult mode, there may be no work to do!

Understanding the importance of attachment

The real finds that helped with the FAIT model came after the initial acceptance of the usefulness of looking to the unconscious. These were John Bowlby, Donald Winnicott and Margaret Mahler. I never tire of studying their work.

Bowlby is well known for his work on attachment. He was able to put the deeper understanding of unconscious processes into everyday language and demonstrate the impact of attachments, broken attachments, and attachment-based therapies. He noticed that children in hospital went into a state of pathological mourning when separated from their parents; he is the founder of open visiting for children in hospital. He led the field in policy development to recognise the attachment needs of children and what can be done to help when things go wrong.

Unfortunately, some modern services have got it wrong. I noticed recently that fostering services for newborns have a policy to move the baby on at age one – based on an assumption that, if they have attached to the first foster carer, they will attach to the next. From my own studies, I would say that this is probably the worst time to move them. They will be only just beginning to look outside of themselves, with no formed solid core until much later.

Bowlby described attachment-based therapy for older children and adults. This is based on therapy sessions at the same time and same place, with the same person, for as long as needed. What happens in the therapy meeting is less relevant than the fact that the session happens. I have known a number of people who can use this as supportive psychotherapy for many years, often only once a month. They have the necessary attachment relationship to maintain their mental health. These are individuals with the basic fault that Balint talks about, who have not attained the depressive position that Klein talks about, and who did not have a secure reliable attachment figure in early childhood. Regular therapy is not available for all who need it and is rarely available for children or for people with learning disabilities. Even most mental health therapy interventions are now limited to 10 sessions. The depth of the need is so often missed. Shimmens and Skelly cover this extremely well in *Love, Attachment and Intellectual Disability* (2024).

Donald Winnicott worked primarily with children and was a prolific writer. His first publication *The Child, The Family, and the Outside World* (1973) described – in great detail –the developmental processes that we all go through. The stages are also the ones measured by the FAIT, which was developed later. Winnicott was able to put emphasis on the role of the primary attachment figure and got into trouble for referring to 'refrigerator mothers' (ie, those who struggle to love their baby and to invest in its development). He was ahead of his time, as we now accept that babies need warm affection and care if they are to thrive – although hopefully we would be more willing nowadays to accept that babies may have alternative carers and it is not all down to the mother to provide everything.

Winnicott blamed mothers for the development of autism and this has been challenged since. A reliable cause of autism has yet to be identified and, in my clinical experience, I have found lots of presentations. Some autistic people have been described as not engaged from day one – babies that slept, did not cry, and did not ever seem to need another human being. Others have been fine until age two or three, when they have withdrawn from contact with parents. It is still a mystery. There was some research that showed an emotional, attachment-based intervention did relieve some symptoms but ultimately we still do not know.

Winnicott's book *The Piggle* (1971) described, in detail, therapy with a very young child who had been traumatised by witnessing her parents behaviour. Using modern models of trauma, we would say that her development was arrested by trauma. Using the psychoanalytic model of unconscious processes, we would say that her experience interfered with the development of the conscious self. It is the same thing. But we are trying to arrive at models that can be widely available and not too complicated for people to understand. We are never going to have psychoanalysis available for all; it is too expensive and not enough people are trained to practise it.

This takes us onto Mahler. Finding her work on 'the psychological birth of the human infant' captured for me that process of accommodating unconscious processes in visible, observable behaviour. With her colleagues, she studied children from birth to the age of five in relation to their primary carers. These were not children with disabilities – although they did identify some children with difficulties.

The main message, however, was identifiable observable behaviour that followed a pattern from birth, with total dependence, through to childhood with a degree of independence. She referred to this independent stage as 'psychological birth'. This equates to the term 'individuation' – ie, a sense of self as separate, a conscious state of being. The usefulness of this study is in the description of behaviours through the stages. They are observable and therefore measurable. Once we have a measure, we can diagnose and then we can see if treatment is possible.

Exploring the impact of trauma on emotional development

Further exploration of the model and experimentation led to the development of the FAIT. Careful study using naïve observers arrived at the realisation that people could observe, and with inter-rater reliability, secure a meaningful answer in 40 minutes. Longer observation did not change the result. The measure arrives at categories of behaviours, so specific behaviours are irrelevant and not influenced by context. An individual can be playing games in one setting, eating a meal in another, following a learning activity, or whatever. It is not what they do that matters; it is the way that they do it. The observation technique and scoring can be learned by most people working in the field, which means that it does not require the constant input of highly trained professionals. It's best if direct support staff get training in the model; once they understand that they are helping their service users or pupils to get their emotional needs met, they thrive.

As soon as the stage of arrested development has been identified, the right emotional environment can be put in place to facilitate progress to the next stage. Some, with the right approach, will reach individuation and go on to live happier, more settled lives. Others will benefit from being provided with emotional support appropriate to their stage of arrested emotional development and will have more contented lives. For some, the trauma that has affected the unconscious processes and delayed the development is huge. However, we do find that all can benefit and show reduced anxiety if their care matches their need. The stage of arrested development in very distressed people often shows them to be less than two years old emotionally. At this stage, they are still very dependent on a 'significant other' safe person to help them to manage anxiety and to function.

The FAIT captures the impact of trauma on emotional development and on that stage before the conscious mind takes over. The work of the psychoanalysts helps us to see what we are dealing with. The reality of limited resources means that this approach is workable, affordable and effective. We can still add therapy to the treatment plan when individuals are ready to talk about their trauma but until then, by providing the emotional environment that matches the stage at which the trauma happened, we can enable people to live happier lives. This works for some of the most distressed people we meet. Their unconscious mind is not necessarily available to them or to the people caring for them, yet there will always be trauma that has interfered with the processing of unconscious material. Finding a way to hold someone emotionally until they are able to face the past is well worth doing. This therapeutic approach, based on sound theory and experience, is the result of study over many years and has been shown to work.

References

Balint, M. (1968) *The Basic Fault: Therapeutic Aspects of Regression*. London: Tavistock.

Berne, E. (1961) Transactional Analysis in Psychotherapy. New York: Grove Press.

Bowlby, J. (1988) *A Secure Base: Clinical Applications of Attachment Theory*. London: Routledge.

Freud, S. (1895) *Studies in Hysteria*. London: Hogarth.

Jung, C.J. (1912) *Psychology of the Unconscious*. London: Kegan Paul Trench Trubner.

Klein, M. (1922) *The Psychanalysis of Children*. London: Vintage.

Mahler, M., Pine, F. and Bergman, A. (1979) *The Psychological Birth of the Human Infant*. New York: Basic Books.

Malan, D.H. (2001) *Individual Psychotherapy and the Science of Psychodynamics*. London: Arnold.

Shimmens, V. and Skelly, A. (2024) *Love, Attachment and Intellectual Disability*. Shoreham: Pavilion Publishing.

Winnicott, D.W. (1973) *The Child, the Family and the Outside World*. Middlesex: Penguin.

Winnicott, D.W. (1971) *The Piggle*. London: Hogarth

Chapter 3: The Story of the FAIT

The foundations

As I reflect on the story of the FAIT, once again I realise that it is almost my life story! The research that led to the FAIT became my doctoral thesis, which was awarded in 2003 (Frankish, 2013). That was the culmination of 10 years of data collection and experimentation, including experimental treatments based on early data. Some of this was written up for publication along the way (Frankish, 1992).

If we go back another ten years, we reach the point where my early work in individual therapy began. The first group of clients was reported on in my 1989 paper, which followed on from my presentation at the International Association for the Scientific Study of Mental Deficiency (IASSMD) in Dublin in 1988. This was the first time I shared a platform with Dr Valerie Sinason. We were treated as the 'alternative to the mainstream' but were welcomed by some. It was one of the editors of the journal *Mental Deficiency* who encouraged me to submit my paper for publication. He was a gem and I have a lot to thank him for. I knew I was seeing something different in my patients but I was just starting out in my career and it meant an awful lot to have that encouragement. The paper was published and well-received. Many years later, I was told that it is a very rare paper on outcomes of psychodynamic therapy for people with learning disabilities.

One of the things I realised quite quickly was that there was no way it would be possible to provide individual therapy for all the people who needed it. From my caseload, I was becoming more and more aware of the emotional issues that needed attention and of the dominance of behavioural approaches in the services I related to.

The old hospitals were still around at that time and I was involved in the closure of several of them. All the planning was practical, with very little consideration of the emotional needs during resettlement or for the emotional issues that were there anyway. Many of the people had no family contact, low recognition of their attachment needs, and no idea what was in store for them. It was, in fact, policy to prevent the development of attachments at that time. I am aware that there is still a policy to avoid the development of attachments in some services. Everything in this book and other similar texts will argue for the need for secure relationships if emotional disability is to be addressed. So many people with disabilities lose their primary attachment figure and have little chance of forming real attachment relationships later in life.

It seemed obvious – and right – that if we could not provide individual therapy for those who needed it, then we should look into a way of providing 24-hour care that is therapeutic. I quickly realised that my definition of therapeutic wasn't necessarily shared. From a medical point of view, medication is therapeutic; from the physio's point of view, meaningful activity is therapeutic; from the speech and language therapist's point of view, meaningful communication is therapeutic; and so on, with nurses and care workers providing the day-to-day physical care. There were never many psychologists and virtually no psychotherapists in learning disability services. At this time, however, services were 'cradle to grave' – ie, the whole lifespan. The switch to separate child and adult services came later, with both positive and negative impacts. I know I preferred working across the full age range, but I chose adult services in the end.

Still pursuing the aim of recognising and treating emotional disability, I was involved in the opening of a small low secure facility in one of the hospitals I had provided psychology services to. The unit was a converted ward and had six patients. We put in place a 'kind parent'-type model for the individuals. We established that the 'parent power' rested in the weekly review meetings and that was where decisions could be made. In the meantime, the staff and patients (I use that term because it was a hospital) followed an orderly day that was planned and predictable, with a named key worker plus named link staff on each shift. I had a pager and was on call overnight as well as in the daytime. The nursing staff, the psychiatrist and the patients adapted well to the regime and all made progress. The model of care began to make sense to all. The person-centred, structured and benevolent approach was a shock at first but gradually made sense as people made progress.

This was probably the beginning of the trauma-informed care model of safe place, safe person, and trained people, plus individual therapy if needed. It worked well but was disbanded with the hospital closure plan. An attempt was made to replicate it but there was a gradual slip back into a hospital model, which was medically led.

I was involved in more hospital closure plans over the next few years and was able to influence some of them to provide services that were aimed at providing emotional support. I continued to collect data and to speak at conferences, looking to spread the word. I was also part of the group of like-minded people who set up a charity to provide supportive living for complex people. This charity is still active and has provided individual care and support for the last group of people to leave one particular institution.

A psychotherapy supervision group was set up at that time, with support from Dr Valerie Sinason. It was within this group that I discovered the work of Margaret Mahler. This became the foundation of the FAIT.

The Institute of Psychotherapy and Disability (IPD) was formed to provide a home for those of us working with the emotional needs of people with people with learning disabilities. Our dream was for it to become a centre of learning, recognition and registration for therapists working in the field. Sadly, that has not been realised but it did become – and still is – a home for those people who provide a psychodynamic approach in their work. I was a key player in the IPD but have settled in retirement for being a supporter. For most of my career, I have provided training placements for psychologists seeking to work in (or at least experience) psychodynamic therapy.

The next stage of the development of the FAIT involved working in a secure setting. The theoretical underpinnings of the FAIT helped me to see that there must be trauma behind the distressed behaviour I was seeing. I was also aware that the people who got locked up when distressed were probably the most distressed of all. It followed, in my thinking, that they must be the most traumatised group. And so it proved to be.

One of the other tools that I have used, along with the FAIT, is the House Tree Person (HTP) assessment. This involves the three drawings and their analysis (more information on how to use and analyse this assessment is available). In the secure setting where I worked, it was possible to use the test at three annual points and analyse them. A captive research group! It was dramatic to find that the drawings on these three occasions were the same for those people who had no therapeutic intervention at all. The people that showed the most change were the ones who had individual therapy. There was a middle group, showing some change, of those who had attended specific group therapies (eg, for sex offending). This work with the HTP confirmed for me that psychodynamic approaches were both effective and necessary.

The research to develop the FAIT involved lots of observations in this secure setting and my previous community setting. There were four assistant psychologists involved in gathering the data. At first, they collected data during quite long observations. I had previously carried out observations for longer periods and in different settings for the same subject and found that the setting made no difference to the findings. It did not matter what they were doing; it was the way that they did it (Frankish, 2013).

Scoring the data was the next issue and there was also the question of continuous or time-sampled data collection. Various experiments were undertaken and it became clear from statistical analysis of the findings that the score could be allocated after 40 minutes of observation, with information on what was observed in 20 seconds, written in 40 seconds, and on to the next minute. It seemed so easy and brief that I continued to question it. I did, in time, accept it was right. What I have found since is that, once experienced and competent in establishing the emotional developmental stage from using the observation, you can be fairly accurate just by watching. You know what you are seeing, and what to look for.

Emotional development stages

The emotional developmental stages are all based on Margaret Mahler's work. She describes six stages but we rarely see Stage 1 or Stage 6 so the FAIT measures Stage 2 to Stage 5. This realisation followed from the hours of data the four assistants had gathered. It felt like a prize had been awarded when I realised how powerful the measure was.

It is possible to summarise Mahler's stages, including those not used in the FAIT. Stage 1 is symbiotic and rarely seen in older children and adults. If a child is so severely traumatised at the beginning that they haven't progressed to the next stage, they will appear to be shut down and non-responsive. I have seen this, albeit rarely.

Mahler's next stage, Stage 1 in the FAIT, is differentiation. During this stage, behaviour is self-referenced, so self-exploratory behaviour is observed. We all have some differentiation behaviours, such as twiddling our earrings, flicking our hair, or tapping our feet. But if these behaviours are dominant, it is an indication of trauma in the first few months of life. We do see a lot of this type of behaviour in profoundly disabled people. This probably stems from the fact that they have never been able to explore the world or make active connections. They can, however, develop further if provided with the correct emotional environment. I could write another book about this group of behaviours and may do so one day. It would make extremely painful reading. Head-banging and skin picking – both distressing to see – usually fall into this category.

As soon as a baby can roll over, we have signs of moving into Mahler's practising stage (Stage 2 in the FAIT). This involves repeating the skill until competent and then adding it to their repertoire, as another skill becomes available. We see lots of practising behaviours in our client group. The stage of development is expected at 10 to 15 months and, if it's maintained beyond that, is indicative of trauma around the age of one. Children without disabilities can get stuck as well. It can present as Obsessive-Compulsive Disorder (OCD), autism, and other signs of arrested development.

Providing the right emotional environment usually promotes progress to the next stage. It may take some time and providing the right support can be a strain. If there are glitches in the provision, there will be regression or interrupted progression. With our trauma-informed care provision, we have seen some dramatic progress to the next stage. It takes some time and this may be related to the age of the people we are working with. In theory, it would be quicker with children who have spent less time stuck in this stage.

If the practising stage is traversed successfully, the next stage is early rapprochement. This is the beginning of meaningful two-way interaction and Stage 3 in the FAIT. If we observe a toddler, we see the change as they both seek and respond to the adults around. They will play games and engage in lots of two-way activities. They are beginning to talk and saying 'no' is a good indicator of the arrival of the stage. It fits with the traditional 'terrible twos', when children get into a confused state about who is in charge. They are struggling with the development of independence, which is both attractive and frightening. We see this stage in secure units, prisons, most therapy referral services, and caseloads. Individuals can be very demanding and definitely need lots of attention to confirm their fragile sense of self.

Moving into late rapprochement (Stage 4 in the FAIT), the sense of self gradually develops and strengthens. There are more negotiated activities and decision-making in co-operation with others. There is more understanding and acceptance of the other person's point of view.

The last stage of emotional development (Stage 6), which we don't measure in the FAIT, is individuation. This is the stage of an established sense of self that is separate from others and acceptably so. An individuated person would not be in need of therapy generally – although, of course, people can have traumatic experiences after individuation and these can have consequences. This would usually be PTSD with a different presentation.

When assessing PTSD, it is possible to differentiate between people who have only experienced trauma after individuation, and those who have experienced trauma on top of early trauma. The treatment approach is different and the outcomes can be evaluated differently. Treatment of PTSD after individuation is usually shorter and can be fully effective. Treatment of people with early trauma can mean a lifetime of supported living. However, people who have individuated but have a cognitive disability will probably need care for intellectual disability reasons. I have used the term 'emotional disability', as I think it describes the condition that follows from trauma before individuation.

It would be beneficial if there was a wider understanding of the emotional developmental stages and their impact on whole life experiences. There is no doubt that these issues do not just have relevance for people with intellectual disabilities but, for people with intellectual disabilities, it is so important to capture this emotional disability model. Using behavioural approaches with 'reward and ignore' treatment plans are wrong and painful. The person who is pre-individuation needs constant positive regard. Guidance for acceptable behaviour is fine; any withdrawal of care and attention is harmful.

The assessment tool

Using this model led to the decision to design an assessment tool to measure the stages of emotional development. This tool is the FAIT, which was published in 2019 by Pavilion Publishing. In the 40-minute observation, it is possible to capture the essence of the person and the need. It is freeing for staff and clients to understand the meaning of distressed behaviour.

In recent years, Positive Behaviour Support (PBS) (LaVigna and Willis, 2012) has become widely advocated for people with intellectual disabilities. It does have value and is recommended by the National Institute for Health and Care Excellence (NICE). However, it can miss the need for emotional support and the provision of a significant other. If asked to contribute to a PBS plan for someone, I usually identify a need as "needs to have confirmation of self at all times", then the instruction to meet the need as "make available a named significant other at all times".

There is a heated debate in some circles around the gaps left by the full adoption of PBS. It will be hugely beneficial when we can produce the evidence needed to establish 'positive emotional support' into NICE guidelines. There are some organisations such as Respond that are taking a lead with this. PBS was preceded by positive programming, and we had an intensive support team in my NHS service in the 1990s, providing input to families with children showing distressed behaviour. It was called challenging behaviour then, but this is a term that I hope has disappeared. We found that there was always a small group for whom positive programming just didn't work, and it was always the distressed group who needed that attention to their emotional needs.

References

Frankish, P. (1992) A psychodynamic approach to emotional difficulties within a social framework. *Journal of Intellectual Disability Research* 36; 559–563.

Frankish, P. (2013) Measuring the emotional development of adults with ID. *Advances in Mental Health And Intellectual Disabilities* 7(5): 272–276.

Frankish, P. (2019) *Frankish Assessment of the Impact of Trauma*. Shoreham: Pavilion Publishing.

LaVigna, G. and Willis, T. (2012) The Efficacy of PBS with the most challenging behaviour. *Journal of Intellectual and Developmental Disability* Sep; 37(3): 185–195.

Mahler, M., Pine, F. and Bergman, A. (1979) *The Psychological Birth of the Human Infant*. New York: Basic Books.

Chapter 4:
The FAIT and the Under-Fives

When we consider the impact of trauma on emotional development, we are mostly looking at adults with learning disabilities who have been misunderstood for many years. They have often ended up in secure facilities, been described as challenging or disruptive, and placed on lots of medication. I want to consider now the circumstances that precede that kind of life story and think about early intervention.

There is a booklet called *Nought to Three – Becoming Me* (2019), which comes with the FAIT. The FAIT is marketed for adults with learning disabilities, whereas the *Nought to Three* booklet talks about the developmental process that gets interrupted by traumatic experiences. These are usually not noticed when they happen, as they are often ordinary events, yet are experienced traumatically by the child at the time. The most common traumatic event for a young child is the arrival of another baby, a sibling, who arrives before the first child has reached the individuation stage of emotional development.

Clearly, not all children are traumatised by the arrival of a sibling but – in my clinical experience – a lot are. If the older child has a disability, there may be even more trauma. If we remember that individuation is arriving at a sense of self as a separate person, then we can see why events before individuation can be traumatic. Without a strong sense of self as separate, with manageable anxiety and less dependent on others to make the world safe, we are likely to react in a way that is not helpful.

Consider the happy healthy two-year-old who suddenly finds a new baby added to the family. The parents who continue to treat the two-year-old as emotionally dependent on them will meet their needs sensitively, while also giving the baby the best start. In those first few months, the older child's needs are greater, as they are at a critical stage of emotional development. They have some level of understanding, they observe, and they react without thinking. They need a lot of help to reach the stage of a secure self. The new baby has lots of physical needs, and requires attention when awake, but – during periods of sleep – is largely self-sufficient.

Parenting is not the easiest job in the world. Balancing the needs of babies and toddlers is not simple at all but many parents manage it very successfully and know almost instinctively how to meet the differing needs of their offspring. Parents who only have one child do not have to face the issue of helping both or all. Only children do not have to adjust to being displaced and think of others. Children with lots of siblings may have to adjust in both directions. It can become a very complex situation, which puts a lot of pressure on parents to get it right.

How the FAIT model can help parents

The observable stages of emotional development measured by the FAIT give insight into the stage that an individual child (or adult) has reached. They also give a useful indication that something has happened if the progress to the next stage is delayed or arrested. Take, for example, a child who was well established at the practising level with some early rapprochement behaviours. They are probably beginning to play two-way interaction games, able to make some choices, and showing signs of preferences for people. The next stage would be more interactions, more engagement, and more reasoning. A new baby arrives and the older child reverts to repetitive practising behaviours, apparently disengaging from contact with parents. This is an indication of trauma and possible arrested emotional development. It is very common for this to happen. If the older child is given special attention and encouraged to interact one-on-one, leaving the baby out of the equation at this stage, they will usually adjust, recognise that the parents are still making the world safe, and continue with their development. By the time the baby has moved into practising, the older child will almost certainly have individuated and be able to assist in the process of socialising with a younger sibling. This is not always a simple process, as all readers with more than one child will know. But being armed with the model of understanding is extremely helpful. And knowing the meaning of observable behaviour is empowering.

The complex processes going on in the developing mind during these developments cannot readily be accessed; however, the simplification of these processes into an observable measure is the essence of the FAIT. It was developed to make life easier for those who provide care and support for people in need. Most parents find a way through and most children do well. However, some do not, and the waiting list for people for CAMHS in 2025 is huge – suggesting that there are difficulties for quite a lot of children. If we have a model in our heads for recognising and understanding that the desynchrony between intellectual and emotional development is an indicator of the problem, we can be empowered. The more we understand, the better it is.

It is vitally important that we understand and accept that trauma leading to arrested emotional development can be caused by very ordinary experiences. As with the arrival of a sibling described earlier, it can similarly be something like a two-year-old momentarily losing sight of their mum in the supermarket. It can be an emergency health issue, like the first cold that leaves you unable to breathe. It can be accidentally eating food that is too hot, or falling over, or any ordinary event that is unexpected and momentarily creates fear. If there is someone there to reassure and make all well, then usually all will be well. But if there is no one there, or the person there is irritated and unsympathetic, it can be traumatising. We have all experienced those moments of stress and distress when we say or do something unhelpful, maybe shouting when we should be reassuring. Children do build resilience and can cope with parents who do not always get it right. What is needed is recognition of an interruption to emotional development, if it occurs, and then an addressing of the issues.

If there is an interruption in development, this can be addressed by treating the child as though they were at the previous stage. This means reducing expectations, accepting more infantile behaviour, and gradually encouraging development to the next stage. This sounds easy and it can be fairly straightforward – although there is a dearth of expert advice around and it can be more difficult, or slower, if the child concerned has additional disabilities.

The need for trauma-informed substitute carers

I have covered families so far, including parents adjusting to help their children to reach a secure sense of self as an individual. In the 21st century, many children are experiencing alternative care for much of the time, as their parents both work. Nurseries and childcare centres vary enormously in their ethos and competence. Ideally, all staff will be familiar with the stages of emotional development. Most are skilled at understanding physical, intellectual and social development; not so many have the additional knowledge and training when it comes to the emotional development that underpins social development. Now that babies are in alternative care before they have any possibility of having a secure sense of self, it is important that staff do understand. The key factor is that each child must have a named significant other as the substitute parent while in care. This factor alone makes all the difference. This is also vital and generally accepted in special schools, where school-age children with delayed emotional development need to know who is keeping the world safe.

There is always a danger that substitute care becomes task-oriented instead of person-oriented. If we are to fully grasp the need to avoid trauma, and to facilitate emotional development to individuation, we must put the 'being with' before making sure that all tasks are done. This sometimes creates questions from teachers, nursery assistants, nurses, etc, who see what needs to be done physically and prioritise this. A nursery that is untidy and chaotic but in which all the children are connected emotionally to an adult is better than one that is neat and tidy but the children look lost.

Ideally, all adults working in childcare will be trained to recognise when they have a child with early trauma and arrested emotional development. If they perceive the stage of emotional development and recognise the need, then they can provide the right emotional environment for development to occur. The benefits are huge. Early interventions are always better than late ones. This leads me to think about the strong young men I have met in secure services, who are aged 18-plus physically but probably intellectually only five or six and emotionally less than two.

They are big and strong and can work out lots of mischief – emotionally, however, they will not be able to foresee consequences and they will continue to test until someone makes the world safe for them. They cannot respond to reason, only to guidance; they cannot respond to a reward culture, as it has no meaning. They only respond to safe, real human relationships that are aimed at providing them with emotional security. Sadly, it takes time and the certainty of continuity. In reality, they are usually moved on so often that there is no chance of providing what is really needed. It follows that identifying the problem before a child is five years old is well worth doing; identifying it when it happens is even better. Prevention is so much better than cure.

Putting these theories into practice

There have been two opportunities for me recently to have an influence with regard to some of the issues that I have spoken about in this chapter. The first was a significant piece of work with a special school, featuring an opportunity to provide some training for the whole staff group. It was possible for them to have regular sessions with the head of support staff and gradually all the staff became aware of the impact of trauma and the impact of providing a secure emotional base for people. The atmosphere in the school changed for the better. There was more tolerance of distressed children, following recognition that it was distress rather than simply bad behaviour. Sadly, one child was moved away to a residential setting because their level of need was too great for the school setting. But there were several children who wanted to stay with their peer group until college age and this was gratifying.

Another example was a commission to provide some training for the staff group at a nursery. This came under the umbrella of infant mental health, something that had been championed by the local health commissioners. This project was very constructive and helpful – albeit sadly not continued, as resources run out. The staff members who attended responded very positively and clearly felt that they were empowered by the knowledge that arrested emotional development does not have to become a permanent state. This is one of the most important things to have come out of this work with emotional disability; the recognition and acceptance that it is a treatable condition and that progress can be made is highly significant.

Another positive thing that came from this piece of work was the personal development of one of the young women who attended the course. She was so impressed with the ideas and recognised the condition in a child that she was supporting, so she enrolled to complete our Level 5 training in disability psychotherapy. This involved a full year of study, which she followed enthusiastically. The child that she was supporting benefited greatly from her increased knowledge and her commitment to their emotional development. This is just one example and it would be good to have the results from a large cohort to establish the efficacy more thoroughly.

Chapter 5:
The History and Development of the Frankish Group of Companies

Inevitably, this chapter and the next will reflect something of a life story for me and my daughter. It is inevitable that our shared history will have had an impact on us. It is useful to consider our pattern of development as individuals, and the theory and practice of therapeutic care, and how this can be applied to people today. We all need to learn from our life experiences and putting that learning into practice is a good thing. There is a vital need to learn from past successes and mistakes. Sadly, memories can be short, with learning getting lost as new ideas take over. One of this book's themes is ongoing reflection on the role of institutions – something that should not be forgotten.

The trauma-informed model of care we have developed comes from a sound understanding of the needs of traumatised people. More importantly, it comes from the knowledge of what works, what can be successful in alleviating pain, and how to progress on the path to a peaceful life. The emphasis is on people with an intellectual disability, but we also look at people with dementia and other disabilities, and reflect on the impact of trauma on all children and young people.

The elements of trauma-informed care that we have arrived at are:

- a safe place to live – one that is not dependent on behaviour;
- the availability of a significant other person to provide emotional security;
- such people to be trained and supported themselves; and
- individual therapy to address the primary trauma when ready.

In order to address these four elements effectively, the model has evolved into four distinct organisations. There is a holding company to provide the safe place to live. It is a requirement of supported living that the landlord and the care agency must be separate. This fits well with the model and avoids slipping into a residential care provision.

The second element is provided by the registered domiciliary care company and again this provides for individual care packages designed to meet specific needs rather than a general care model. The emphasis is on familiar people forming real relationships to provide the 'significant other' role. For the purposes of demonstration, in this story we will refer to Amara Care.

The third element is provided by specific training and staff support sessions, led by psychology and counselling staff. The training includes the 'All Behaviour Has Meaning' concept, covering behaviour from a behavioural, cognitive, psychodynamic and systems perspective. Staff are then able to identify the meaning of the behaviour in the person they are supporting, and from there they are also trained in the use of the FAIT. All staff need to complete this training in their probationary period. They need to fully understand their role as the significant other. Frankish Training has online courses relevant to the model readily available. It includes 'Train the Trainers', which Paula Levett talks about in Chapter 8.

The fourth element is provided by psychology and counselling staff. Individual therapy is provided when the person is ready; the therapy varies in frequency and depth. Some people can only talk when walking, whereas some need quiet space indoors and others need text contact or email every day – whatever is indicated needs to be provided. Therapy must be person-centred and individually led. It is not easy to provide this element and it is very hard to convince commissioners of services that they should pay for the psychology input. The psychology staff have to bring in income from other work to cover the cost of providing this necessary element. In the past, it was normal for specialist care providers to buy in expert psychological support. Now they are not required to do, so they do not.

At one time, we had a team of psychologists providing consultancy and therapy services to several learning disability and mental health facilities. We also provided a valuable service to parents with a learning disability who were pursuing court cases involving their parental rights. Legal aid was stopped for this group and so most of these parents are never assessed now. This must surely contribute to the increase in the number of children in the care of local authorities.

Prior to setting up the group of companies to provide the specialist service, we had previous experience with other organisations. Some of that history is covered in other chapters. It is worth considering here why the present model is a group of limited companies. This follows from legal restrictions, which are not always helpful. Some of the issues are discussed in Chapters 6 and 12.

Ideally, all would be provided within a charity model, but the charity would still need all the elements to be provided and the necessary financial support. There is already a charity that was developed on this journey and follows some of the model; it was involved in the re-provision for a hospitalised group as part of a hospital closure programme. The charity was also able to design buildings to cater for specific needs and create care plans to meet individual needs, with significant success.

Being a trustee of this charity was very rewarding but could not, of course, provide a wage. At that point, I worked for the NHS and pursued the charity work in my own time. Eventually, after retirement from the NHS, it was logical to start the group of limited companies. There is more flexibility, even though the limited companies model limits the financial benefits that follow from being a charity and a social housing provider. As a private provider, we cannot access full housing benefit for the people we support – placing quite a strain on finances. We acquire suitable properties and these are the right fit, but this puts financial pressure on the system.

The overall model needs to be robust if it is going to survive over time. It could be franchised but will always require a degree of altruism to make it work. Big profits are unlikely to ever be made, so this model does not appeal to the big investors. Putting the needs of the people being supported first comes at a cost. There needs to be the willingness and ability to make a phone call at ten o'clock every night if that is what is required. There needs to be a willingness to keep repairing the shower or the radiator if that is what is required. There needs to be tremendous patience and willingness to keep going for the long haul.

We have shown that the model can work and work well. It grew from work in individual therapy (Frankish, 1989), which could never reach more than a few people, to a therapeutic care model to reach more people. It needs to grow further to reach even more people. This does feel like an evolutionary process; it needs to evolve further into mainstream policy.

When I consider how our provision has grown and its theoretical underpinning, I am aware of the layers that evolve. In the centre is the person with trauma. They need to be surrounded by a cocoon of safety. That cocoon of direct staff and location needs to be held by a strong organisation (or group), which – in turn – needs to be held by the legalities and funding. The legalities and funding come from the government and need to be clear in policy for health and social care, as well as mental health policy.

This holistic model must be the way forward if we are going to be able to alleviate the distress of traumatised people. There is, perhaps, some possibility of services for people with intellectual disability; it would be good to extend this to others. There is a mental health crisis in the UK at present. Finding ways to facilitate emotional growth and maturity can only be a good thing. We must always remember that we are talking about people who are traumatised in early childhood before they have formed a strong sense of self.

The small venture of our group of companies has shown what can be achieved. One of the key takeaways is what can be achieved by frontline staff with support. For the most part, it is useful to have the support of fully trained professionals, but sometimes it is not. One of the pressures on our services has come from professional staff in local teams who lack a background in emotional development and emotional disability. Ideally, all professional training would include a module on emotional disability – even exposure to the primary developmental model for all health and care workers would help.

Thinking about things from the psychoanalytic point of view, it is possible to see why certain things do not happen. Unfortunately, we all have trauma in our lives. On a positive note, that is a leveller and defines who we become, to a large extent. However, on the negative side, we all have to defend ourselves from the pain of our own experiences. This can insulate us against being able to think productively about trauma and trauma-informed services.

There is a lot of talk about trauma-informed care that makes no sense to me. Most people will only be able to consider trauma that has taken place after individuation, which – in psychological terms – is the process people go through as they form a distinct, separate identity. This misses the point for the very distressed group that we're talking about, who have been traumatised at an earlier age. Our automatic defending against the pain is understandable. But we need to face it and work with the underlying core issues if we are to be effective.

Other chapters will expand on these ideas. There are stories of practical applications, stories of personal development that has eased people into tolerating pain and helping others, and there are real attempts to explore the issue of history and the fact that legislation that does not always help. Regulation is needed but sometimes it is so hindering of progress. The rules and laws that govern supported living are not easy to navigate. The Care Quality Commission has restrictions that mitigate against individual plans that can work. The boundary between supported living and residential care can be confusing and unhelpful. Repeated reorganisation of the NHS and social care causes confusion and delays.

One way of looking at the problem is to see that the system itself is traumatised. We live in times of stress and uncertainty. The world feels under threat from climate change and over-population. Our country feels less settled than it was, with political uncertainty, financial pressures, and threats from technology. If we are to be able to support and help those in need, we need to be able to adjust to our own pain and look beyond ourselves.

If we consider the developmental model for our care services, we can see that establishing the old hospitals was a symbiotic stage that was followed by very physical support, as in early childhood. All found ways to function at the practising level, then gradually parted company through rapprochement (again, in psychological terms, this refers to the culmination of steps taken by an infant from symbiotic union with the mother towards an established sense of separateness and personal identity). If the hospital closure programme had truly represented 'individuation', all would be well, but quite a few people still need care and support – perhaps not in big institutions but, rather, in individual care packages that address their needs. We have shown this can work for some very fragile and distressed people.

This care model needs to be more widely accepted and used, together with the appropriate legislation to make it easier to put together. There must be an end to the attempts to pass financial responsibility between the NHS and social services. One of the features of the hospital rehabilitation programme was a dowry system, whereby each person was allocated funding for their future care. Allocating a fund for an individual based on their assessment of need would potentially free up some of the service plans. It would, however, require the assessments to be good enough and the money sufficient. There is the risk of a perverse incentive emerging, whereby big companies build big institutions to accommodate lots of people who have their own dowry. Maybe it is better to try to be more individually based in the assessment and provision.

Our group of companies has developed and grown in response to need and based on our own experience gathered over a lifetime of provision for people with intellectual disabilities and complex emotional issues. The experience of the old long-stay hospitals has coloured our thinking, in the sense that we do not want to go back there. Some people still consider that the safety and reliability of that old service model was better. For some, it was – they were fed and clothed and did not have to work. However, the main things missing were real human relationships, warmth, and recognition of individuality; I do not think we want to go back there.

This book is about stories, lots of different stories about people and organisations that have contributed to the knowledge base of emotional disability. There is still, it seems, a long way to go before we have full recognition of a holistic, personalised approach to services for people who have experienced trauma. There is still a huge battle over what is needed to prevent the consequences of traumatic experiences in early childhood. The psychoanalysts have been talking about this for years, yet we still struggle to make progress. It does seem that one difficulty is the contrast between something that can provide a quick fix – akin to taking antibiotics for a chest infection – and an approach that is, or can be, lifelong.

Reflecting on my experience through the NHS, charitable work, and the development of the group of companies that we have now, I can see that there is a way forward if only the powers that be could see it and adopt it. I reflect on the quality of the research that was done at the time of the hospital closure programme and regret that a lot of it has been lost. Service development has varied and we seem condemned to not learn from past mistakes and maybe that is part of the human condition. Trying to look holistically at whole-life solutions for people who have whole-life conditions has led me down this path. It is possible to develop the ideas further and we have set up a Community of Practice, which will hopefully spread the word more widely. Some of the contributors to this volume are members of that community and anyone reading this now is welcome to join. We meet online on a quarterly basis to share experiences, questions, and ways forward.

When Amara Care first started (it was first registered at the end of 2003 but became operational in 2004), a company called Pat Frankish Associates existed, which was my psychology company. We had intended to put everything into one company but this plan immediately encountered difficulties in terms of insurance, as insurance companies were not prepared to insure companies that offered a wide range of services. We have found, all along the way, that there are obstructions to what we consider to be logical thinking. The people and organisations involved in risk management always seem to be looking for ways to avoid risk altogether, rather than ways to manage it. Given that we have always worked with more complex people, there will always be more risk. I can see why locked units have developed, in the same way that prisons have expanded, as a way of putting risk in a safe place. But, sadly, all that happens is that the restricted units increase and nothing – or very little – of a recuperative nature takes place.

Forty years of my own experience as a psychologist has helped me to see what can be achieved if the right support is offered at the right time in the right way. The development of Amara Care and Pat Frankish Psychology was the first step towards trying to do this. We have had some success but could have had more if the support from commissioners and the legalities concerning insurance were more straightforward.

From those initial beginnings, we went on to purchase a property within which to provide the model of care that was advocated at the time. The story of the first property, Rowan House, is included in Chapter 6 and written by our co-director who is also my daughter, Amanda. This leads into another legal issue – namely, the need for property to not be owned by the same person who is providing the care, unless it is residential care. As supported living is the model that we were advocating, this was not appropriate and thus led to the formation of yet another company, called PF and AJ Holdings. This company now provides the properties for the holistic care plans that we provide. Amara Care still provides care and support to people living in properties that we do not own. The psychology company still provides psychology and counselling to people who do not live in our properties. The holistic care (where we provide a property, support services, training, and therapy) is the main part of what we provide. It is necessary to be holistic in our business model if we are to provide all the elements, some of which are not fully funded.

During the past 20 years of provision of the model, the psychology company was commissioned to provide a service to local special schools. This included staff training, staff support, and some individual therapy for children. This was very effective and was evaluated at the time, showing a decrease in difficulties for the children, as well as an increase in staff confidence and the general feeling of competence. This input was funded by the local NHS commissioning group but was discontinued when the funding run out. One of the schools involved received accolades shortly after this input, for their services to the children concerned, which was an indicator of the school's continued competence.

From the beginning, the aim was to recognise why children struggled with their behaviour, see their distress, identify their stage of emotional development, and put in place the appropriate regime. The results were very positive. And some were very quick. One young person was able to respond to a suggestion of putting painful things in a box to be brought to the next session to talk about. After their session, the young person found that things in the box ceased to cause pain and functioning improved dramatically. Another profoundly disabled person who cried a lot was able to respond to a support programme that recognised that they were more able intellectually than they were emotionally. Once the emotional needs were met, the functioning increased, including increased use of their electronic communicator. It reminded me of the work I did as an undergraduate to design a talking machine for a young person with severe cerebral palsy.

I feel the need to note the element of chance involved with so much of this. When we consider the policy decisions by successive governments, we can see that there has never been a comprehensive shared understanding and provision. Dr Valerie Sinason, in her book *Mental Handicap and the Human Condition: New Approaches from the Tavistock* (1992), is able to talk in some detail about the difficulty that we – as a society – have in facing the issue of difference. People with disabilities and complex needs are a challenge to all services and there are not enough of such services to ever come to the attention of mainstream service planning. I remember my father referring to them as 'the Cinderella Services' and this does still seem to be the case. There is much talk nowadays about the crisis in acute health services and, of course, these services cannot be ignored. But they take up so much attention that there is very little energy, it seems, left to channel into addressing minority groups who have the same intense level of pain.

I am struck always by the impact of trauma on individual development, but also by what could be achieved if the trauma was recognised in early childhood. Some children get the support that they need and do very well. Others are not identified until they are much older and, if they're not identified until they are adult, they're often difficult to help because they are bigger and stronger than the people trying to help them.

Alongside the development of service provision, there was another piece of work exploring the possibility of setting up a master's degree-level course in disability psychotherapy. We were invited to do this by Doncaster College, which was seeking to become a university at the time. This has now happened but, sadly, the master's degree in disability psychotherapy has yet to. We continue to explore the possibility that it might. The course included seven modules, looking at individual, group and systemic approaches, and entailed a fairly comprehensive exploration of all aspects of disability – something that is, or seems to be, not very well understood by a lot of people.

The grouping together of people that used to happen with the institutions can still happen, leading to a loss of individuality. Everything in this book is about being person-centred and recognising the meaning of behaviour for each individual that we're trying to help. By recognising very early trauma and the impact it has on the development of personality (the 'real self'), we can provide people with a therapeutic process. If this is well matched, then there will be some resolution of the early trauma, along with a significant improvement in the quality of life for the individual.

If the disability psychotherapy course had come to pass, there would have been an opportunity for more professional staff to understand better and therefore be able to support frontline staff providing a trauma-informed model of care. Within Frankish Training, we have continued to offer the course modules but are of course unable to offer a qualification. We still have some optimism that it may one day come to fruition and be made available to more people.

The strapline for Amara Care is 'Supporting Meaningful Lives'. The aim is to do this for all who receive our services and all who work for us.

References

Sinason, V. (1992) *Mental Handicap and the Human Condition: New Approaches from the Tavistock*. London: Free Association.

Frankish, P. (1989) *Meeting the needs of handicapped people: a psychodynamic approach*. Journal of Mental Deficiency Research, 33:407-414.

Chapter 6: The Rowan House Story

Amanda Brock

This chapter is about my own growth and that of our flagship service, which was provided in a house where many of our clients were tenants. As a director, I brought my experience of working with people with learning disabilities in many different settings to the company. I had been involved as a support worker within a local long-stay hospital – working on the wards and in the activity centre – and in several residential home settings for people leaving long-stay hospitals. I have also worked at local day services for people from long-stay hospitals and now work in a tenancy support model. All my work has been with the most challenging and severely disabled group of patients, clients and tenants. As the daughter of Dr Pat Frankish (a consultant clinical psychologist and author of this book), I have been guided by using her knowledge and expertise to support me in my roles as a support worker and – later – in management.

Beginnings

As a child I lived in and, later, regularly visited a long-stay hospital for people with mental retardation (as it was called then). My grandparents lived on site, as one was the hospital unit manager and the other a ward sister. I have a lot of memories of being with disabled people and this is where I gained my first work experiences. My first job on leaving school and before going to college was in an activity unit and on the wards of the hospital. This was supporting the most disabled adults and children, who either had challenging behaviour or were profoundly disabled (or both).

I got to know the people, as I used to visit the hospital on open days and had spent time on the children's ward assisting at mealtimes. I witnessed how people were supported in the hospital. My mum worked at the hospital, on the wards and in the adult education unit, where I also visited and played games with people. There used to be a film night and our local school would put on talent shows and pantomimes for the patients to watch.

All this gave me a social understanding of how people with learning disabilities were treated before the Community Care Act of 1984 (formerly known as the Registered Homes Act of 1984) led the process of closing the hospitals and moving such people into the community. This was also the place where Pat Frankish started her first psychological job. Based on my own experiences, I continued to want to do better for these people. I believe strongly that anybody can do what they want to do if they have the appropriate support.

After college and travelling, I relocated to work in a small group home for four residents who were moved back to their own community following a hospital closure. All four had severe learning disabilities and challenging behaviours. This gave me my first experience and knowledge of running a small group home in the community and of the challenges this entails. During my time there, I worked with an assistant psychologist who was gathering observational evidence by using what is now called the FAIT. This was part of the research in support of Pat's doctorate. I also supported the individual who was the subject of Pat's paper, which was published in 1992. The research showed that, by providing a significant other (as recommended by Donald Winnicott) and a safe base (as recommended by John Bowlby), those with severe learning disabilities grew emotionally. The key was to provide consistent staffing and be there to build an emotional attachment, regardless of whatever behaviours were being displayed.

I was also a key worker for a person who had been abused and wore several pairs of trousers to keep themselves safe. Through being consistent, the team helped the person gradually come to trust that it was only necessary to wear one pair of trousers. The other type of work we did involved the Bereweeke step training system, a behavioural skills teaching method. Having psychological input was essential to help staff and clients develop.

I relocated again and worked for a short time at another home for six clients with learning disabilities before joining social services to work in day services. I had a specialist role with those who required occupational therapy and physio support and worked closely with speech and language therapists. I progressed to a Grade 2 support worker.

With my knowledge and for my own development, I decided to go back into group homes and became a registered manager for four homes, housing 12 residents with severe learning disabilities who had come from a long-stay hospital. This was my first managerial job and I soon became familiar with the difficulties of managing staff, budgets, local authorities, and social care settings. It was challenging. I learned a lot about different conditions and that my skills and knowledge were better suited to working with people who have severe learning disabilities and communication difficulties.

The closure of another hospital gave me an ideal opportunity to share my knowledge from my entire background. The project did have specialist input from clinical psychologists, nurses, occupational therapists, physiotherapists, and speech and language therapists; this was a typical multidisciplinary team for people with learning disabilities. By this time, the observation technique to use with the staff team was in place there, and the clinical psychologist also knew Dr Pat Frankish's work. From observations and using an intensive interaction model, we saw small developments in those who had been traumatised by being in hospital and having to be moved into the community.

Having done this for a few years, I was seconded to work in the NHS to set up a support service for people with disabilities. The role involved talking to those with all kinds of disabilities and forming a charity, with the aim for it to be run by disabled people. This was an eye-opener, and diplomacy was required to make it work. I didn't go back after my secondment, as I moved to another area and took up a registered manager post again – albeit in a six-bed home for people with challenging behaviour.

This time, I was working for a private company, where I learned how to work with people who had Prader-Willi syndrome alongside people with learning disabilities and challenging behaviour. I introduced star charts for behaviour, created daytime tables, enabled residents to go to college, and built up activity plans with the staff team. I turned the home around, transforming it from a chaotic institution into a more structured and stable environment for those living there, by providing significant others and a safe base for the residents.

The knowledge I had gained from working within the NHS, social services, and the voluntary, charity and private sectors enabled me to feel confident in setting up a company and particularly looking at what we could provide in social care. I soon started looking to purchase a residential care home and found one locally, which we purchased in September of that year. This would become the story of Rowan House.

Creating Amara Care

In 2004, Dr Pat Frankish and I came together and started the domiciliary care company, which also marked the start of moving all my mother's work and research into a new era. As she mentions in the previous chapter, we worked with a local college to develop an access course in disability psychotherapy. The course detailed information on several therapists – in particular, Sigmund Freud, David Malan, Margaret Mahler, Pat Frankish, Valerie Sinason, Donald Winnicott, John Bowlby, Carl Rogers, Patrick Casement, and Melanie Klein. The ultimate aim of the course was for our staff team to learn about the need to form emotional attachments and be able to see that all behaviour has meaning. This course, titled 'All Behaviour Has Meaning', has four elements – namely, a behavioural approach, a cognitive approach, a psychodynamic approach and a systems approach to working with people with learning disabilities.

By learning about all the separate therapists, particularly John Bowlby and Donald Winnicott, staff were able to provide a safe base. We see that this is provided by our holding company. Then a significant other is provided in the form of our care company. We then have psychological support from our psychology company and provide training through Frankish Training. The Frankish model was developed and staff were taught how to do the observations, meeting clients' emotional needs. Over the years, this has become known as the FAIT.

Rowan House was purchased as a family home unit but registered as a residential care home. An old farm building on a smallholding, it had four horses and was registered to deliver riding for the disabled. There were also lots of other animals – all of which required looking after. Whereas the previous owners had lived on-site, we altered the property to run the home for the benefit of the residents, not for the proprietors. There were six residents and about 50 individuals who stayed over on respite throughout the year; hence, a lot of responsibility. There were four staff employed and one volunteer who looked after the animals. We needed more overnight staff. Until we could employ more staff, I spent many hours living in and got to know the residents very well.

At the time we took over Rowan House, the government White Paper *Valuing People* (2001) looked at how services were provided for people with learning disabilities. Based on this and the directors' experience, we knew early on that those living at Rowan House didn't need residential care and we decided to register the property as a 'supported living' facility. At the time, the government had put a lot of money into providing supported living services but the local authority was not interested in our proposed changes. We were not able to call it supported living, so we called it a 'tenancy support' model. All people living there became tenants on an assured shorthold tenancy and had their care provided by the domiciliary care provider.

While we waited to de-register, we put a planning application in to develop the land into a holiday location where people visiting the area could stay as a family but leave the person with disabilities to be supported throughout the day, enabling them to go off to the seaside. We wanted several log cabins and a caravan park but all was rejected by planning on account of being in an area at high risk of flooding. This risk changed from 100 to one to 50 to one overnight. Twenty years on, we're happy to say that there has never been a flood, but the plan was lost.

The process to de-register was a difficult one. As previously stated, the local authority did not support the move but the Care Quality Commission (then Nottingham Community Housing Association) did. Lots of meetings and assessments took place for the people living with us. Two people were transferred into another residential care setting, while the others remained and had their support purchased individually. They had their own flat and front door key, enabling them to grow. Unfortunately, those tenants that attended day services had it stopped overnight, as they no longer lived within a residential care setting.

Over the years, there have been several models of managing the service that fit with the Frankish model incorporating the FAIT. Initially, we had three flats and an activity centre. We had a separate staff team for each flat and had the equivalent of a warden on site to manage the property. The model enabled those being transferred to have the chance to start to cook their own food, go out more, and engage in doing what they wanted. As this progressed, we employed indoor and outdoor activity co-ordinators. The outdoor people looked after the land and the animals and put on gardening and animal care activity. The indoor co-ordinator provided activities inside, such as arts and crafts, cooking, bingo, and educational activities. During the indoor activity, we provided a meal at lunchtime. This was cooked by some of the tenants with support. This is where we introduced daily living skills and cooking but also table manners and how to behave within a social setting. All the skills learned within our activity centre enabled the individuals to grow in their own self-acceptance and integrate more within their community.

As mentioned earlier in this chapter, in 2006, we began working with Doncaster College to provide an access course in disability psychotherapy, which some of the staff from Rowan House attended. Part of the course involved performing the observations on the tenants in their home, which was the start of actually assessing individuals. We had already been using the model by providing the services of a secure base and a significant other; soon, we began to see how people were developing in themselves and becoming able to make real choices in their lives.

In 2007, the company started a Level 7 (master's-level) course in disability psychotherapy. The course took four years to complete and I completed it. We had a trainee psychologist work for us and we also set up a group with all the tenants who we supported (and their staff), which they decided to call a 'friendship group' and which ran for a couple of years. Within this time, we discussed all sorts, but a recurring theme was that of 'moving on'. In 2009, we enabled four of the original tenants to move into houses within the community, allowing us to offer places in Rowan House to more people. The process has continued for the past 16 years.

The next move we made was to develop training courses so that the people we supported could gain qualifications. We registered with the Open College Network to run Level 1 and Level 2 courses in independent living. These enabled clients to gain individual accredited qualifications relating to domestic skills, educational skills, and horticulture. This meant many clients received credit for all the hard work they had done in developing themselves, but the staff were also rewarded in the sense of seeing how they had helped people to develop. These were exciting times as people grew, developed, and moved out of Rowan House. We supported the development of further homes and were open-minded when it came to offering Rowan House to new people. The model was working to the extent that we provided the secure base (ie, Rowan House), the staff by Amara Care, and the psychological support and staff training in the Frankish model by Frankish Psychological Services (now Frankish Training).

Alongside the Level 7 disability psychotherapy course, we ran a Level 4–5 course in which the managers of our company participated. When they did the course, part of the role was to use the FAIT (2019) in assessing individuals but they also had to run a small group – all of which was supervised by one of our consultant psychologists. This was an enabling group, in which all staff were included. We saw the benefits of being there week by week for 20 weeks in how the participants developed. This nurturing was what enabled people to build up the confidence to say what they wanted to do.

The next five years we spent nurturing skills and it felt rewarding to see people's further growth. Some individuals moved back to Rowan House but this was mainly due to health reasons, as they needed 24-hour support. Other tenants went into a smaller environment in a house living in the community; for some, this was less space than Rowan House, given that their only personal space can be their bedroom. This wasn't enough for some people, as the rest of the home was shared areas. When people did move back to Rowan House, the process continued, and what we have found is that those with autism are the ones that struggled more in the community setting and needed the nurturing environment of Rowan House.

Around 2017, funding seemed to change, and the local authorities began to show interest in the clients they were funding and who should have been supported by social workers. Up until then, there had been little input and fees had stayed the same since the shift in 2006. The clients were reviewed and we were told we couldn't move people unless the authority agreed, so this slowed down our process of enabling them to grow, as we couldn't move people if they wanted to transition to 'normal' living. Therefore, we had people stay where they were until placements broke down. What we did find was that when people left Rowan House, they gradually stopped wanting to return for courses or day activities and started to live their own lives around their own property, which was a clear sign of moving on to being more content in their own space. Others were happy to remain at Rowan House indefinitely.

In 2019–20, COVID-19 hit us and everywhere else. It affected how we managed services but one of the good outcomes of living at Rowan House was that everybody came together. Initially, we all found it difficult but – as the restrictions were made on us all – the running of Rowan house changed. Instead of being segregated on their own, clients spent more time together. The staffing was reduced at times, so it was difficult to monitor the structure, but we all came together more in the home and it was run like a residential home for a while. This did affect different characters in different ways and some began to shine. It enabled individuals to gain the strength to voice their opinions. They used to role-play going out and about and doing what they wanted to do – to the point that three clients decided they wanted to move on and into a more independent property (ie, their own house).

Alongside the model being used within services, I can see that the companies have also worked through the four stages of Margaret Mahler's separation-individuation process seen in early childhood – namely, the differentiation phase, the practice phase, the rapprochement phase, and the consolidation phase – and alluded to in the previous chapter:

1. When we started Rowan House and when we take on new clients, it is akin to being at the symbiotic stage. The company holds the client as they get to know the service. It can take about three months for a bit of trust to start developing between the person and the company.
2. The client then moves into a differentiation stage, in which they start taking control of the environment a little and notice that they live somewhere else and within a team. As we go through this stage, the staff team get to know what is required within support plans and rotas to help the person grow into the next stage of their tenancy. The tenancies are usually an assured shorthold tenancy for six months.
3. As the person moves through this stage, they reach the practising stage. This is where a little more routine begins to emerge, as we get to know the person we are supporting and how they fit within the model.

4. The client then moves into the early rapprochement stage, wherein they start asking questions. At the preliminary assessment stage, some people will already be at this stage emotionally. However, during the tenancy, they move through to late rapprochement – ie, when they know more about what is required for themselves. This may be the time that we enable them to move on to another property because they've outgrown the support provided at Rowan House.
5. If the client moves on, you could say that they then have reached the stage of individuation from Rowan House. Thus, the individuation–separation process is complete. Then we introduce more people, which starts the process again. This can be demonstrated by all the people we have supported at Rowan House, as described next.

The first 18 months of us having Rowan House was when it was a residential care home. Originally, the clients (or 'residents', as they were called at that time) did not do anything for themselves. We were strangers to them when we took over Rowan House. We held all seven that lived there, as if in the symbiotic stage. As we got to know each other, people started to show that they could do things for themselves. They quickly moved through to the practising and early rapprochement stages. Some individuals attended day services away from Rowan House, which is equivalent to going to school. When the decision was made, and we de-registered the residential care home, we all rebelled and wanted our own independence. This was our first time of seeing the cycle.

Our next stage was having the three flats and the activity centre. This was all new to everybody and so, once again, we entered a symbiotic stage. We held each other in the face of the changes and quickly moved through to everybody practising how to be with the new set-up. We also had two new individuals move into the home. As people became confident with the new arrangements, they moved through to rapprochement. Through the aforementioned group we facilitiated, some individuals spoke up and wanted to move into a new home in the community. When this happened, they moved on to a new home and re-started the process in that home. Rowan House clients at that time continued to live at Rowan House and new people moved in, thereby starting the process again. This process has continued on and off throughout the past 20 years.

There was a gap in the usage of Rowan House when a crisis arose in the form of water coming through the ceiling and we had to quickly find everybody somewhere else to live. Everybody then had to get used to a new house, which felt like a return to the symbiotic/differentiation stage. Once all the clients established where they were in the community, some individuals rapidly became more independent and started going into the community on their own. In the meantime, Rowan House underwent some refurbishment, then two new clients moved in and the activity centre was used as a cafe for the community.

When the original residents moved back to Rowan House, they had grown in their own development to the point most were nearing late reproachment. However, one of the original people who moved into Rowan House was still at the differentiation/practising stage, and this did not work. It demonstrated to us that mixing individual people with learning disabilities when they are at different stages of emotional development as measured by the FAIT does not always work. The environment does play a significant role, as well. Getting the balance right and providing all the elements of a therapeutic environment is essential if resilience is the goal.

Rowan House Timeline

2004

Rowan House is purchased as a Residential Home for six residents and respite for about 50 individuals with a learning disability.

2006

Rowan House is de-registered and transferred to three flats with a daytime activity centre as a supported living / tenancy support model of support. All tenants have an assured short-hold tenancy. Wardens were employed to manage the property.

Commenced Training in Access course in Disability Psychotherapy that staff from Rowan House attended.

2007

The service developed to have indoor and outdoor coordinators providing activity for those living at Rowan House but also external people. Warden is removed.

Commenced level 7 Disability Psychotherapy. Rowan House tenants and those attending day activities involved in group psychotherapy which they called a friendship group.

2009

Five of the original tenants at Rowan House move into two different properties in the community and Rowan House is backfilled with new tenants.

Developed accredited courses from the Open College Network (OCN) in independent living. Managers undertook level 4 and 5 courses in Disability Psychotherapy.

2010 – 11

Tenants moved into another property in the community, and vacancies were backfilled.

2014

One of the properties rented in 2009 is closed and the tenants move into other properties.

2015

Two new properties rented and two tenants from Rowan House move.

2017

Social Care funding changed, meaning people started to be funded for what they needed and started to develop their skills more using community facilities.

Rowan House closed due to flooding and tenants were relocated. Once the property saved, two new tenants move into Rowan House but it is left empty for nearly a year waiting for referrals.

2019 – 20

COVID 19 hit and the provision moved to become more residential throughout the lockdowns.

Another property rented and two of the original tenants from Rowan house move into this adapted property.

2024

Current tenants in Rowan House move to another property and new tenants move in.

References

Freud, S. (1895) *Studies in Hysteria*. London: Hogarth.

Malan, D.H. (2001) *Individual Psychotherapy and the Science of Psychodynamics*. London: Arnold.

Casement, P. (1985) *On Learning from the Patient*. London: Tavistock Publications.

Rogers, C. (1951) *Client-Centred Therapy: Its Current Practice, Implications and Theory*. London: Constable.

Mahler, M., Pine, F. and Bergman, A. (1979) *The Psychological Birth of the Human Infant*. New York: Basic Books.

Winnicott, D.W. (1973) *The Child, The Family and the Outside World*. Middlesex: Penguin.

Bowlby, J. (1988) *A Secure Base: Clinical Applications of Attachment Theory*. London: Routledge.

Sinason, V. (1992) *Mental Handicap and the Human Condition: New Approaches from the Tavistock*. London: Free Association.

Frankish, P. (2019) *Frankish Assessment of the Impact of Trauma in Intellectual Disability*. Shoreham: Pavilion Publishing.

Chapter 7:
The Property Story – A Historical Perspective

This story begins with the old long-stay hospitals and how people came to call them 'home'. The Victorians, I am sure, meant well when they designed and built these buildings. Some of them were second-generation workhouses, some were purpose-built, and some were converted from stately homes. The message was clear, however, that people who are different cannot be in open society. They must be shut away out of sight and, for many people, that meant out of mind too. I'm going to concentrate on the learning disability story because, although there is a similar one for people with mental health issues, that is a bit different.

My own early experience was with Caistor Hospital in Lincolnshire. It was built originally by a local benefactor as a 'house of industry'. The benefactor concerned wanted to make sure that people who were destitute had somewhere to live in exchange for doing some work; one of the jobs was to chop firewood. One building was called a 'vagrant's ward', which was eventually altered into a nurses' home and then turned into a private house where I lived with my family. After the house of industry was made into a workhouse, and when that became the usual way for society to look after people who could not look after themselves, it became the responsibility of the community rather than the individual. There was a board of governors who were responsible for the running of the workhouse.

With the formation of the NHS in 1948, the workhouse became an institution and later a hospital. It was never very big, with a maximum number of beds of 220. At the time that Caistor Hospital became a health provider, it was noted in the records that there were people chained to the wall and there were clearly people who could not manage themselves. This became the precursor to the delivery of a service to people with intellectual disabilities, who were known at that time as 'mentally retarded' or 'mentally deficient'. My mother went there in 1938 to train as a nurse to the 'mentally subnormal', as they had become known by then.

Caistor Hospital was initially women-only, with children but no adult males – although later a small group of men were admitted. The central ward was the old workhouse, with two other wards of a similar age. A new children's ward was built in the 1950s, along with four staff houses, followed later by another two wards and an activity centre. Eventually the staff houses became 'patient' accommodation, where patients would reside prior to their move to the community. There was always a plan for Caistor Hospital to house the more disabled people.

The 1913 Mental Health Act provided the legislation for the institutions, later called hospitals after the NHS was founded in 1948. The development and registration of professions followed; there were roles for doctors and nurses. The qualification my mother was awarded was registered nurse for the mentally subnormal, which was the term that followed 'mentally deficient' but preceded 'mentally handicapped' – the latter being in use when I first became involved. Before 'deficiency', there were terms such as 'retardation', 'imbecile' and 'moron'. 'Mental handicap' was followed by 'learning disability' and now 'intellectual disability'. Dr Valerie Sinason has written poignantly in *Mental Handicap and the Human Condition: New Approaches from the Tavistock* (1992) about the name-changing avoidance strategy. This is part of the property story, in that it enabled people to be categorised and therefore put into large groups.

The early institutions were usually built or converted from large buildings that were somewhat secluded, rather than in the high streets of the towns. The message was always that their inhabitants were to be 'out of sight'. I think of Aston Hall in Derbyshire, which had been a stately home, and of Harmston Hall near Lincoln, which was a manor house and the sister hospital to Caistor. All were off the beaten track and designed to maintain separation.

The criteria for being moved into one of the institutions were defined by the Mental Health Act of 1913. Women who had a child out of wedlock could be called a 'moral defective' and institutionalised. People who were a bit slow could be diagnosed as 'feeble-minded'. Other often quite dehumanising terms included 'spastics', 'Downs', rubella damage, and birth injuries. Buildings were often drab colours, with solid fuel heating systems, and not very warm. There were no incontinence pads or nappies. The dining room that I remember had duck boards on the floor so the urine and faeces could drop through the slats to be cleaned up after everyone had gone.

It was not uncommon for wards to accommodate 80 to 100 people, with 12 inches between beds, which was just enough room for a small locker that held any personal items. I remember making up bundles of clothes at night – not personalised usually but, rather, just a set from whatever came back from the laundry. One set each; impersonal and drab. Laundry was operated by the patients under the watchful eye of a member of staff, given that the more able patients worked in the laundry and the kitchen or maybe even cleaned wards.

As the history of the institutions grew, so did the institutions themselves. There seems to have been enough money to keep building new wards. More people were being confined to the hospitals and probably more seriously disabled children were surviving, but perhaps society was becoming less tolerant. My first experience of a mental hospital was Rainhill Hospital near Liverpool; it had 2,000 beds. There was clearly a policy of 'out of sight, out of mind', but the financial resources must have been there to support the continued expansion.

There were lots of patients who worked in the hospitals, doing menial tasks for small financial rewards. Many of those people would have a diagnosis today of autism or a personality disorder. They were able to function in the closed environment of the hospitals whereas they would find the demands of open society too complex. Sadly, many of them were taken advantage of. They were all vulnerable people but, because they were kept out of sight, most members of the wider public were unaware of the situations.

Then there was a revolution, signalled by the commencement of the hospital closure programme. JP Martin and D Evans' book, *Hospitals in Trouble* (1984), gave an account of inquiries into several hospitals.

The level of physical, sexual, emotional and financial abuse that was discovered was huge. Inquiries led to the Community Care Act of 1984 and the closure programme. The new Mental Health Act led to different criteria for admission to hospital and the new Education Act said that all children had a right to an education. Initially, schools were set up in the hospitals, but then special schools began to appear.

There was a lot of discussion about transferring financial resources. The money from the hospital closures was meant to be enough for the alternative provision of services; it was not, and never has been, but at least it made a start. The building of special schools is another part of the property story. Identifying available land and resources led to another set of legislation. Most service provision fell under the remit of local authorities but the resources had to come from central funds initially. There is a constant and recurring theme of this type of transfer not being resourced well enough, followed by arguments between government departments as a consequence.

Emerson, McGill and Mansell (2001) led some comprehensive research studies in the 1970s and 1980s, to support the transfer period. They were able to show that if the more complex people were properly provided for, the others could live a fairly ordinary life in ordinary houses in ordinary streets. Authorities varied in how they delivered on this. There was a marked difference between those areas that had a hospital closure (and hence the financial transfer) and those that had never had an institution. The latter areas tended to be more innovative in their provision for people 'coming home'. In the former areas, a lot of big houses were set up by hospital staff, providing residential care for 10 to 20 people. These were, effectively, 'mini-institutions' – albeit with an opportunity to go out and about in their local community if they weren't too isolated.

Some of the people from the old hospitals did move into ordinary housing. They usually moved in together in small groups, so there was an expectation that they were content to live together. It was known from Emerson (2001) that some people needed single-person services, however, and it was never easy to secure the finances to provide this. Personally, I got involved with the closure of 10 hospitals during my career and sometimes was able to advocate for some individually designed schemes. Some were amazing; most were good enough.

A significant part of the work was done by the charity Mencap and the British Institute of Mental Handicap (BIMH), as it was known then. Brian Rix, a famous actor, led publicity campaigns, heading up Mencap and gathering public support. Mencap still provides lots of property for people to live in, as well as a full range of support services and a strong political voice. The British Institute of Mental Handicap became the British Institute of Learning Disability (BILD) and took a lead in publications, training and campaigning. The BILD was based in the converted old hospital in Kidderminster, Worcestershire.

Both Mencap and BILD continue to be influential and both these large charities were built on – and rely on – the families of people with intellectual disabilities. Some of my initial training before I went to university was at BILD. I remember 'music and movement' sessions and the positive impact they had on the people in the hospital. It was the beginning of positive input alongside the existing warehousing model. However, it took some time to close the institutions and provide ordinary housing, and this process is still not complete.

One of the positives offered by the hospitals was the groups of people therein who could be studied for research. Some very valuable insights gleaned from them were written up by people such as Joan Bicknell (1983). I remember her talking about 'the psychopathology of handicap' and capturing the impact on families of having a child with a disability. She also spoke and wrote eloquently about the effect on disabled people of the life experience in institutions. Joan could move an audience to tears with no effort. I see her history as similar to my own and Dr Valerie Sinason's, only a bit earlier. She was very outspoken and her words are still relevant today.

There continues to be uncertainty concerning the housing of people with disabilities. There are some wonderful purpose-built facilities for some, whereas others are having to slot in wherever there is a vacancy – often having to share when they are emotionally not ready to do that. The financial support has never been enough. The arguments between health and social care are destructive and harmful; the 'estate' belongs to health and was not all transferred to social care. The financial support for the appointment of nurses did not transfer enough to social care, community teams kept lots of the old buildings, and lots of nurses became community nurses or became managers of small group homes.

It has always fascinated and annoyed me that people with disabilities get moved into shared housing and have to 'earn' the right to their own place. This is completely back-to-front. The emotional maturation model indicates that they need a single-person service first and then may graduate to sharing, if they have the opportunity for therapeutic care that aids maturation.

There have been some village communities over the years and the Botton Village charity is still alive and well. L'Arche, a Christian organisation, is also providing services for people with intellectual disabilities. It is unlikely that either of these, or similar provisions, can provide for the complex traumatised group. Dr Valerie Sinason's father developed Ravenswood Village many years ago and Valerie talks about this in her chapter. The US state in which we provided training (see Preface) uses the village model now.

And so it continues today. The property side is complex but the lack of sufficient funding for the traumatised group needing single-person services has led to the development of the next generation of institutions. Known as low and medium secure units, they are not yet as big as the old hospitals, but they are isolated, closed and institutional. They are mostly health-funded and run by medical staff. They use up a lot of money. I was involved with one development where the houses were changed from eight beds to nine, as the ninth bed equated to the profit. But nine meant there was always someone left out and the emotional impact was significant. This unit closed soon after it was established.

During one of the hospital closures I was involved with, we managed to buy two new semi-detached properties and put in an access door to enable one member of staff at night. As it was a new build, we also had the bedrooms made the same size – with a box room for sleep-in staff on one side and a staff office on the other side. This provided an ordinary house on an ordinary street for four people. It does not take a lot of imagination, but it does need financial resources to be available at the initial stage. It does not work for the social worker looking for a bed immediately and the 'vacancy' model does not work very well either. Designing a service from scratch is best.

Identifying an appropriate property to rent and then appointing a specific staff group to train up for a specific complex individual has to be the best model. Casting around for a vacancy in an established group home will always put an emotional strain on everyone, putting the system under stress and potentially causing setbacks for the established group. Working with the whole group of staff and tenants can sometimes help the system to cope and thrive. What usually happens is that one room becomes a revolving door as new people come but then don't settle and so have to move on.

When looking at the 'All Behaviour Has Meaning' training, it is useful to look at this situation when studying the systemic approach. The same authority that supported the two semi-detached properties also agreed and funded a later scheme for more people to have purpose-built properties that met their needs. One potential complication is identifying a new tenant who needs the specific design when it becomes available, so a bit of forward planning is required in terms of adaptations to buildings. Sadly, it is often difficult to get all the right people in a room to make suitable decisions. We all know how stressful moving house can be. Finding an existing property with all the desired features can be a challenge. But we do it for ourselves, so we should be willing and able to do it for people with complex needs.

I look at the design of modern buildings and consider the changes in property that I have witnessed in my lifetime. There is still so much effort put into designing buildings and things, instead of designing the care and support that would enable distressed people with trauma in their lives to have what they need. It is possible to design and provide appropriate homes for everyone. Walls can be made punch-proof, electrics can be hidden, and water can be controlled. But, more importantly, individuals who are very destructive can be helped to connect with the world and other people. Managing is not the same as treating. Putting distressed people together with other distressed people is likely to make things worse.

I came across an interesting book, *Evaluating Health Service Effectiveness*, written by AS St Leger, H Schnieden and JP Walsworth-Bell in 1992. This grapples with the conflict of interests between buildings and people; the debate goes on and on. In acute services, we see demands for more hospitals. Similarly, we find community provision is all about vacancies and "Is there a bed?". The right way to be effective for traumatised people must be person-centred and provide safe relationships in whatever building is available – in other words, ordinary houses and bungalows. Grouping together, which is what the system promotes, detracts from what is actually needed and ties up resources in the property instead of the people.

Another big factor is timing. Providing what is needed before individuals become too big and strong to manage in ordinary housing is critical. The shift to separate services for children and adults with special needs has not helped with this. The referral of an adult-size 18-year-old who is traumatised and distressed can be daunting. Identifying the trauma a few years earlier could make a huge difference – not only by presenting an opportunity to build the right property but, just as importantly, by providing the right emotional support during the planning stages. I think of a very complex young man I worked with who had early trauma but then became very traumatised by the move from junior to senior school. It was generally agreed by the multidisciplinary team that he needed a single-person service, with reliable significant people to support him, in order to accommodate his emotional needs but also to help him grow emotionally and have a better quality of life.

The situation now in 2025 is that some of us know what is needed but the resources aren't always available to make it happen. Building properties that are fit for purpose can be quite expensive. But, if they provide an appropriate environment within which people can thrive, it must surely be worth it. Building institutions is only starting the cycle all over again. I hope I have been able to provide a property story that illustrates what is possible and what must be avoided.

References

Bicknell, J. (1983) The psychopathology of handicap. *British Journal of Medical Psychology* 56: 167-178.

Emmerson, E. (2001) *Challenging Behaviour: Analysis and Intervention in People with Severe Intellectual Disabilities*. Cambridge: Cambridge University Press.

Martin, JP. and Evans, D. (1984) *Hospitals in Trouble*. Oxford: Blackwell.

Sinason, V. (1992) *Mental Handicap and the Human Condition: New Approaches from the Tavistock*. London: Free Association.

St Leger, A.S., Schnieden, H. and Walsworth-Bell, JP. (1992) *Evaluating Health Services' Effectiveness*. Milton Keynes: Open University Press.

Professional perspectives

Chapter 8:

Experiences of Using the FAIT Model in a Children's Specialist Learning Disability Service

Paula Levett

I am a Principal Clinical Psychologist working in children's services for over 20 years, mostly with children and adolescents with a moderate-to-profound intellectual/learning disabilities. I am currently working in a specialist service for children and adolescents within a learning disability service, which is in the unusual position of not having a Child and Adolescent Mental Health Services Intellectual Disability/Learning Disability (CAMHS-ID/LD) provision in the county.

I was originally introduced to the FAIT model by Dr Pat Frankish (Frankish, 2016) whilst working with one of my colleagues (clinical psychologist Dr Amanda Shackleton) in adult LD/ID services, when we were negotiating the support of a young person transitioning into the adult world and across our services in the north of England. During our conversations about this young person who had experienced multiple adverse childhood experiences (ACEs), Amanda – like me – identified that working in a solely behavioural way (this was in the days before PBS had even taken off) was not quite meeting the needs of the individuals who in fact required an approach that focused on their emotional needs. She spoke about the FAIT approach by Dr Pat Frankish, which did consider a person's (or child's) emotional needs. From this conversation, the FAIT approach has subsequently helped me shape my practice with young people and their families as well as endeavour to influence some of the services I have worked in and with.

My training and experience

My own training journey started back when I worked in a CAMHS-LD team in the north of England and completed training up to Level 6 with Frankish Training. This provided me with a robust background to the use of a psychodynamic lens with the children, young people and families I worked with, as well as helping me to think about some of these ideas with my colleagues from multiple professions and agencies.

As I was developing an understanding of the FAIT model, this also coincided with a move to another staff team, predominantly staffed with learning disability nurses and with no specialist mental health provision at that time. At this point, I considered how to introduce the FAIT approach as a potential team-wide assessment that would help us capture the additional elements of the emotional needs of the young people we were working with. I have been very fortunate to work within a team who are advocates for the young people that we support and always exploring ways in which to include the voice of the person with a learning/intellectual disability.

So, while we started to simultaneously develop our skills and knowledge of PBS, exploring what the underpinning values meant to our practice as a service, I noticed that the team were all very aware and open to the idea that there was more to our work than just the mechanics of the PBS framework and approach.

As a team, we explored together how the FAIT model – alongside our PBS framework – was a potentially accessible way to capture the emotional and psychological experiences of the young people we were working with. So, my next task was to explore with our service leads the possibility of training our team as a whole, thus turning this into a team approach.

Putting together a business plan and a training proposal is usually a bit of a challenge in our NHS services; however, I was again fortunate enough to be supported by my managers and we set out a training strategy within our local team in the use of the model and the assessment. We provided the training to the members of our team, and repeated this training a few years later, so new recruits to the service could also make use of this approach. In addition, one of our special schools agree to host the venue – so a few key educational staff also joined the training and, as such, promoted a wider acceptance and understanding of the FAIT approach with our partners.

As the model was more widely and routinely used in the service, our partners started to ask about training for themselves – as well as referring directly to our service for a FAIT assessment – to help develop their understanding of the particular issues some of their young people were experiencing. This prompted me to apply for funding within the organisation to undertake the 'Train the Trainers' course, which I completed along with one of my colleagues who is also jointly trained as a learning disability and mental health nurse. We have now extended our training offer to all new starters in the service to ensure it is part of our team offer.

At this time, we also reflected on widening the training offer to some of our multi-agency colleagues (eg, key staff from the special schools and specialist children's home provisions that we work with closely), who already had an awareness of the assessment but would be in an ideal position to help embed the principles of the approach into the culture and practice of their provision.

Similar to the Frankish Training, our training covers:

- the theory and principles that underpin the FAIT;
- how to complete the observation, scoring and interpretation of the FAIT;
- how it all fits together with other models and assessments used in LD/ID services for children;
- an evaluation to determine that they had taken in key aspects of the model; and
- completion of a FAIT observation and subsequent assessment report (that they presented anonymously) to evidence they had fully understood the principles of the model and were able to share the findings – ie, to agree they had met the appropriate clinical standards.

When developing the training in order to help attendees practise scoring and interpretation, we accessed a YouTube clip of a young person engaged with an adult in intensive interaction. This was a useful exercise to complete in the training room, demonstrating how – for individuals with learning/intellectual disability – cognition and chronological age can differ from emotional developmental stage (ie, considering Donald Winnicott's model of the Desynchrony of Development (Winnicott, 1985). It also helped showcase the importance of attunement and, as this model attests, emotional availability of a key adult to support the emotional development of the children and young people we work with (Frankish, 2016). This clip also indicated which settings were more conducive for children – ie, giving consideration as to whether completion of the observation would be too intrusive for the child.

We also suggested clinicians might need to set expectations for others in the observation setting (eg, if taking place in a school, you might have other children or teachers who may want to approach and talk to you in the middle of the observation or, if in the child's home, it may feel overly intrusive for the family to have a professional 'observe' within their family home). We ask clinicians to consider factors that may change the dynamic for the person being observed, much as you would with any other clinical observation undertaken. Although Dr Pat Frankish's research suggests that the FAIT can be conducted in any setting and obtain the same findings, clinically it is important to ensure that we can maintain dignity and respect for the child being observed.

We also considered the helpfulness of providing basic awareness training to various staff groups in our partner agencies who may come across a FAIT assessment report from our service, so that they have an awareness and basic understanding of the model, which can help them be more open to the findings and recommendations the model asks of them. This also provides an opportunity to make links in their own practice, such as:

- social care colleagues having support and understanding of the need for adjustments to care packages for young people so that they have access to safe, predictable and trauma-informed care; and
- teaching staff reminded about the importance of a relational approach in the classroom.

In this way, the assessment recommendations are more likely to have success and be carried forward in a meaningful way if other professionals supporting a child and their family are aligned with the FAIT model of care. An additional outcome to be considered, with increased understanding from the adults supporting the young person, is that – rather than another 'report' in a drawer that is not used or understood – the professionals can set goals and targets across multi-agency systems, in order to work on improving relationships, promoting exploration and supporting engagement at the right level for the individual child.

Dotting the i's and crossing the t's of governance in our team

Following in-house training, my colleague and I offer follow-up consultations to support staff and ensure their clinical practice and delivery of the FAIT assessment and model is consistent and reliable. The consultation might involve supporting clinicians with issues around reliability of scoring, report-writing, or offering support following feedback to families or other professionals of the findings from the FAIT assessment. The consultation could support clinicians with any further issues required around re-formulation – for example, when identifying 'stuck'-ness from the adults or organisations supporting the child, as well as thinking more about bespoke recommendations that fit with the needs of the young person or the possibilities in their environment.

The process of embedding the FAIT model into the service led to the development of a robust plan to:

- ensure all our team had access to knowledge about the FAIT approach by:
    - setting up a rolling programme for new starters; and
    - developing a refresher course for those in receipt of training more than five years ago, also supporting inter-rater reliability; and
- agree on governance structures by:
    - developing report templates (both professional and more accessible, easy-read versions);
    - producing clinical guidance for clinicians (eg, considerations when completing the observation assessment, or when or when not to use the assessment); and

- developing information leaflets that explain to parents, children and professionals the process and underpinning theory of the FAIT approach, where clinicians are considering using this approach (this was developed in response to feedback from our families and colleagues in other services).

Throughout years of using the FAIT model within our service, we have noticed that there are times when families' services have self-referred for a FAIT assessment, but there have also been some challenges in terms of understanding what people think they are asking for versus the reality of what is really being asked. By way of example, the assessment findings – if not explained and presented clearly – are at risk of being misunderstood, in terms of a child's ability, without a skilled clinician sharing the findings. Additionally, in learning disability services, professionals are aware of the importance of helpfully sharing concepts and findings in a way that is sensitive to the recipient; hence, our team are encouraged to make use of adapted communication and easy-read versions to ensure communication needs are captured when sharing information.

The idea of developing a clinical standard and report template came about as I noticed a wide variation in the way my colleagues were reporting on the findings of FAIT assessments and reflected how this might impact on the children and families. As such, our guidance asked them to consider the following questions in the report:

- Is there a clear explanation to support understanding of the FAIT model?
- Do readers of the report understand the importance of the recommendations and how this can affect outcomes for the child in the future?
- How applicable or bespoke can the recommendations be made for the individual to ensure the report is more meaningful?

Currently, the FAIT model is embedded within our team culture and recognised as a valuable assessment tool that is complementary to other assessments, as well as within our holistic approach to understanding the needs of children with LD/LD.

Informing formulation and intervention

As mentioned, I have observed the use of the FAIT model becoming embedded into the culture of our team, and it soon became understood that as a service we could use this approach to offer a different perspective on a child's experience. Our team was receiving referrals for a 'Frankish/ FAIT' from some of our colleagues and from special schools – and even parents started requesting this assessment specifically – and so the FAIT approach became embedded onto our language and culture, both within the team and by others accessing the team.

I have noticed that the clinician supporting certain children – especially those with high levels of ACEs in their background or those who have experienced multiple house moves – would seek to undertake multiple different assessments in the hope that this next one will be the answer to the child's needs (ie, there was a drive to 'fix' but also some avoidance of formulation). Often I have observed that the clinician is struggling to understand their role in supporting the child but reflected that they also are possibly struggling with the unconscious pain and trauma experienced through the transference relationship in such situations – ie, when a client unconsciously redirects feelings and desires from past relationships towards their therapist, often leading to strong, positive or negative emotions.

I have found that using the FAIT assessment as a starting point and using a consultation or formulation space can help support the wider formulation and understanding of the transference and counter-transference (ie, the therapist's unconscious feelings influenced by their client) being experienced. In such cases, an appreciation of potential counter-transference has helped the clinician step back and see the impact of trauma for a child and how this transfers across the systems supporting them. Using the FAIT, the clinician has been open to sharing a deeper understanding with the child, family and wider professional network of their basic need for a secure base and secure haven from which to process the trauma not even necessarily verbalised within a professional network.

The drive to 'fix' that the clinician is experiencing is mirrored in the professional network and so using the FAIT approach to highlight the unmet need for a young person's emotional development has been found to be the crucial shift in the network's approach. For children with high numbers of ACEs, moving away from a behavioural focus is therefore also crucial and we have found that – along with using the FAIT approach – this helps to steer network conversations towards improving the quality of care and then the quality of life to improve outcomes for the child. As such, using the FAIT can support confidence in the formulation of a child's emotional development needs.

I have also wondered whether delaying the complex task of formulating was associated with delaying 'breaking the news' of the child's level of emotional development, echoing the pain of 'breaking the news' of the original learning/intellectual disability diagnosis. There may be some unconscious avoidance on the part of the clinician of the pain and distress that families and support staff may experience when presented with the idea of the child being at a much younger stage of emotional development than they had consciously considered. It can be important to pay attention to and support staff and clinicians in identifying their own attachment history and help them make links with how this can unconsciously impact their practice. I wonder whether this could also be indicative of their own psychological barrier or defence, highlighting avoidance when having to do painful tasks such as 're-breaking the news'.

Our team offers a weekly staff PBS debrief session and a multidisciplinary team (MDT) case formulation session to provide additional space to process some of the difficult events or chronic 'stuck'-ness experienced. This includes a space to process others' trauma and recognise moral injury (ie, psychological harm from actions that go against the individual's moral or ethical beliefs). Often a case discussion will focus on the use of restrictive practices in one setting but not in others. (NB: We know that the use of restraint can re-traumatise individuals when they have already experienced trauma in their life (Heyvaert *et al*, 2014)).

The MDT group recognised that a solely PBS approach doesn't work for all children and often these PBS debrief or MDT sessions express concern that the voice of the child and their distress is getting lost. One example highlighted where it was clear that one setting saw adults meeting the child where the child was at (in terms of the child's emotional development) – for example, the child was engaged in to-and-fro activities such as playing with balls and rolling toy cars – but staff members were actively engaged in the activity with the child. The staff members were actively creating a secure base by being emotionally available and encouraging the child to explore their environment but also demonstrating that they simply liked being with the child, authentically enjoying the interaction.

In another setting, the child was excluded from interacting with their peers owing to historic concerns about risk, so the child became increasingly isolated in this setting. The MDT group were able to support their colleague to make use of the FAIT approach to keep the child's emotional needs in mind while also revisiting Tier 1 elements of the PBS framework, such as the Capable Environments Checklist. This refers to ensuring that a child/person is supported by people who actually like the person and are able to demonstrate warmth and empathy and interact frequently with positive engagement (McGill *et al*, 2020).

Our team occupational therapy lead emphasised that when we move the focus from behaviour to occupation, we can see how some of these children experiencing restraint or restriction in specific settings were in fact at risk of 'occupational deprivation' (ie, a state where individuals are prevented from engaging in meaningful and necessary activities owing to factors outside their control, potentially impacting their well-being and identity). As such, the child does not have access to sufficient and appropriate activities if their emotional stage of development is not understood as being significantly younger than their chronological or cognitive age. A couple of decades ago, the term 'environmental enrichment' was coined and it seems that – without a model such as the FAIT to keep our focus on the emotional development of people with learning/intellectual disabilities – we keep returning to the same problems of unrecognised trauma and diagnostic overshadowing of distressed behaviour (Emerson and Hatton, 1994).

Cathy Harding, in her chapter in *Trauma and Intellectual Disability* (2021), raises concerns about a culture that fails to support staff in developing 'relational security' and the concern that 'clients become too attached' to the people supporting them. She highlights the risk for people with learning/intellectual disabilities of re-traumatisation if we do not think about trauma-informed care when considering their wider needs. My hope is for our team (and your team) to continue to make use of this valuable reflective space, so we are empowered to highlight and recognise the emotional needs of children disseminating throughout the system supporting the child, in order to ensure we meaningfully consider their emotional development.

The FAIT tool is specifically for people with learning/intellectual disabilities and, in particular, for the hard-to-reach and hard-to-treat population (Frankish, 2016). In our team, there have been occasions when colleagues have spoken to me about how they have attempted to complete the FAIT assessment but have found it hard to score. As such, we have identified that sometimes these children either have borderline or no learning/intellectual disability and their primary diagnosis may be autism.

There might be occasions when older children have in fact reached the stage of individuation but their emotional development is still behind their cognitive and chronological development. At this point, we have often wondered about an alternative method of assessing their emotional development and have recently introduced the Scale of Emotional Development – Short (SED-S) to our teams' practice, which has helped us think about some of our older children or less complex children (Sappok, Zepperitz and Hudson (2022)). By way of example, we recently had a direct external request for the team to assess a young person who was much more able verbally and cognitively, but their experience of developmental trauma had a significant impact on their functional ability. Our social care colleague requested the FAIT assessment; however, we identified that the combined use of the SED-S, assessment of adaptive functioning, and a trauma-informed approach had the effect of directing the social care team towards a more holistic and trauma-informed care plan to support the young person.

Working with families

When I first started using the FAIT tool in my work, I was struck by how the assessment opened up conversations about attachment with parents without them experiencing guilt or becoming defensive about their parenting. Many parents described how this assessment had supported their understanding of their children's emotional needs and were able to translate this into a wider understanding of their child's behavioural presentation. Some parents reported that the approach felt quite intuitive to them and that they understood their child needed to be thought of as much younger in their emotional development without wanting to hold the child back or prevent positive risk-taking to promote their child's development.

I found that developing bespoke recommendations together for their child, depending on the stage of emotional development identified, helped some parents quickly adjust small changes into their approach that fit with their child's needs. By way of example, working with parents following difficult hospital experiences with their child often left them all feeling quite traumatised. Using the FAIT model, I saw how the approach helped parents understand how their child had taken steps back in terms of emotional development and often some of their skills for daily living. One parent reported that understanding where their child was currently at with their emotional development helped them know how to re-adjust their support, acknowledging an increase in the confidence to promote their exploration, with reassurance that their child could still feel safe. The outcome for this child was a successful transition at school and reinforced confidence for both parent and child.

Some of our team members have reflected on managing parents' or other professionals' experiences of taking on board finding from the assessment – for example, when working with:

- a family who is afraid to talk about the emotional world of their child;
- parents who are upset about the use of the word 'trauma', as it conjures up images of abuse that their non-verbal child is unable to communicate; or
- families who struggled to accept their child's degree of disability and are struggling to accept the degree of additional need.

Other parents may struggle with the idea of the learning/intellectual disability itself as 'trauma' and may have experienced considerable painful criticism early on in the child's development from professionals before the disability is formally identified or diagnosed. There are a number of circumstances where a family may find conversation about attachment and emotional development difficult and that it reignites an earlier pain. I spoke previously about times when clinicians may not want to reactivate this feeling for parents and families. However, it is equally important to offer a space for them to process their own experiences in order to bear hearing others' pain.

I have noticed occasions when the FAIT assessment and the sharing of the assessment findings is the intervention in and of itself. Yet, on other occasions, further work is required for families – for example, supporting families around their acceptance of their child's limitation or the longevity of the impact of learning disabilities, which Joan Bicknell spoke about in the 1980s (Bicknell, 1984).

Working with special schools or care providers

I facilitated a training session that included clinical and special school staff. The group was able to reflect on the importance of joint working and common language in combating other systemic barriers (such as financial barriers, lack of resources, lack of shared understanding of a model, and the risk of holding a uni-professional lens). As a group, we explored a wider understanding of the issues faced by the young people we are working with and considered the above-mentioned barriers when sharing the FAIT-informed recommendations.

The group understood that the approach required sign-up from all agencies supporting children. As such, following our training session, the group were promoting joint working to ensure colleagues understand the value of providing a secure base and emotional availability as well as considering the impact on staff in the ways that they meet the emotional needs of the young people they offer care to. We have future plans to offer FAIT training to local respite providers and children's homes for disabled children, which are providing direct care to the young people we work with and are well placed to embed these practices.

Developing a relationship with special schools in our local area has been key. When first introducing the FAIT model some years ago, we commissioned Frankish Training to provide our second batch of training and this was hosted by one of our special schools, who included key staff in this training offer. This has increased the openness to and awareness of the FAIT across special schools in Devon. As we have continued to use this tool, there have been an increasing number of requests from these schools and other organisations working with children with learning disabilities, asking specifically for a FAIT assessment to help them think about a child's needs.

We currently have two clinicians in our team completing the 'Train The Trainers' course with Frankish Training and, as such, have delivered several training sessions that have included key staff sent by a couple of our colleagues in the special schools. We have a growing number of requests from various schools to support them in accessing the training and have found that increasing access to the FAIT approach has resulted in a shared language and appreciation of a trauma-informed approach, so we are pushing against an open door.

One of our colleagues in a special school has moved their staff from developing behaviour plans towards developing young peoples' 'relational plans', thereby thinking about meeting their emotional needs. Their approach has been to support the class team with a wider understanding of the importance of a key emotionally available person, the quality of this relationship, and supporting the child at their stage of emotional development – rather than only focusing on the behaviour. This approach clearly has a strong alignment with the FAIT approach.

Our colleague worked with me to develop a support plan for a young person with intellectual/learning disabilities and complex developmental trauma needs stemming from an early history of neglect. The class team had requested a review of the PBS plan and I offered a consultation to explore this further. I reflected with their class teacher that the reactivated behaviours of distress had escalated in response to a change of school site as well as class teacher (ie, their safe place and safe person had changed), which had disrupted their experience of a safe base. The class teacher was able to shift from a behavioural to a relational position, and we reviewed and repeated the FAIT assessment, recognising that the young person's behaviour was an expression of their emotional and relational needs.

We also agreed with the family carer and class teacher to complete the SED-S assessment, developing a comprehensive set of recommendations for the class team to work on to support the young persons' emotional needs. It was found that, by the end of the first term, the young person was more solidly located in the early rapprochement stage and showed improvements in the development of their communication – meaning we were finding more helpful ways of getting their needs met. The staff group and family carer reported that this was a more appropriate and helpful approach, as it moved away from the behavioural approach to explore the child's attachment and emotional development in a guilt-free, open manner.

I have found it important to consider the existing culture or level of understanding of trauma-informed working prior to developing training when sharing with schools or care providers in order to determine the degree of additional support they need. I have also noticed that training individuals in an organisation, without senior management sign-up, can lead to a risk of staff becoming isolated in their attempts to use this model in their organisation. By way of example, there can be senior or managerial challenges regarding the need for additional support staff, as financial repercussions or worries about a child becoming over-attached can act as barriers.

I have frequently observed during training sessions or when working with individual children with colleagues in special schools that one of our colleagues' common responses when we identify that a child needs an 'emotionally available' person to support the child moving to the next stage of emotional development is to highlight concerns that this "is not in the school budget" or within the remit of an EHCP (education, health and care plan). Providing space to talk about the systemic and organisational barriers in the form of cost implications, staffing or processes, helps us think collectively about how we can work together in order to make sure that those individuals who could offer emotional availability to children would be supported in their workplace.

I noticed that these systemic barriers prevented the organisational decision-makers from thinking about children's emotional needs and connecting with our recommended intervention to support emotional development in the same way as they would allocate time in a class or educational setting for work on communication, sensory processing needs, occupational or physiotherapy needs. Additionally, the special schools and care organisations that are already seeing the value of the FAIT approach are those organisations that have keenly taken an offer of training and have demonstrated the importance of understanding young people's difficulties alongside their emotional developmental needs.

This leads me to thinking about how to compassionately approach my other colleagues – holding in mind their experiences of systemic barriers – to help them explore the possibilities of naturally embedding some of the principles in their work. This would be with a view to showing them the potential impact on a small group of children, which might in turn help them realise the potential and value of finding additional investment of time or resources, in order to see improvements in the children we are working with together.

I aim to continue conversations with our local education and care providers, offering an introduction to the FAIT model for managers and head teachers to support their understanding, with a view to reducing the impact of systemic barriers. This would need to account for potential organisational trauma (Treisman, 2022), such as:

- increased reported moral injury and sickness rates;
- recruitment retention becoming problematic; and
- worryingly high levels of reported secondary and vicarious trauma, compassion fatigue, and burnout.

It will be helpful to:

- recognise the support that staff in our partner agencies require;
- think about how they are carrying, for example, the transferred difficult feelings and associated psychic pain;
- think about their defence mechanisms, such as projection or avoidance that perpetuates some of the systemic barriers to some degree; and
- moral injury that managers and staff might be holding onto.

I have noticed increasingly higher rates of children with learning/intellectual disabilities being supported by private care providers in order to maintain a life at home. The challenges of working with care providers will be familiar to those of you who work with adults. It can be a challenge to determine the level of understanding of or training in trauma-informed care and work within these parameters. By way of example, there is – at times – resistance to buy-in of the FAIT model, similar to the barriers identified with education in terms of the short-term cost of resources and staff. I have found that making use of the multi-agency team around the child is a helpful forum in which to widen the lens and enable providers to consider the longer-term benefits of meeting a child's emotional needs to a child's well-being.

Conclusions

Overall, I have found that by introducing the FAIT model into our service offer, it has added to the team's ability to open up a holistic picture of the needs of a child and the importance of considering their emotional development. It has increased the opportunity for crucial but sometimes difficult conversations with parents around their child's emotional development and attachment, hopefully without triggering feelings of guilt or reactivating past traumas.

However, it is also important to offer clinicians and educational or care staff the opportunity for a reflective space to reflect on and manage their anxiety around talking about a child's level of emotional development. There is the worry that this will open up a 'psychological wound' or re-trigger a latent trauma. I have also found that – as it increases awareness of developmentally appropriate level of care – support can be delivered that meets the child at 'just the right' level to match that need.

I find that, as I continue to think more about the use of the FAIT model, I think about how to integrate its use with the wider system supporting the child, alongside the privilege of training immediate and external colleagues. I have reflected that – although I have enjoyed sharing the ideas and concepts underpinning the FAIT model – I am increasingly struck by the impact of the wider systemic and political arena that rears its financial or resources head, putting systemic and structural barriers in the way of supporting the emotional development of our children.

As I continue to deliver the FAIT approach to children and their families and other supporting adults, I will continue to think with my colleagues more broadly about navigating the barriers to using this type of approach. I will also continue to make use of and be attuned to the wider psychodynamic theories that will help to support our colleagues to navigate through these barriers and maintain their energy in doing this, as well as continuing to keep the young people's emotional development at the centre of our formulation and thinking.

References

Bicknell, J. (1984) The psychopathology of handicap. *Annual Progress in Child Psychiatry and Child Development* 346–363.

Emerson, E. and Hatton, C. (1994) *Moving Out: The impact of relocation from hospital to community on the quality of life of people with learning disabilities*. London: HMSO.

Frankish, P. (2016) *Disability Psychotherapy: An innovative approach to trauma-informed care*. London: Karnac.

Harding, C. (2021) *Providing Emotionally Aware Care in the Positive Behavioural Support Framework*. In Beail, N., Frankish, P. and Skelly, A. (Eds.) (2021) *Trauma and Intellectual Disability: Acknowledgement, Identification and Intervention* (pp. 103–119). Shoreham: Pavilion Publishing.

Heyvaert, M., Saenen, L., Maes, B. and Onghena, P. (2014) Systematic review of restraint interventions for challenging behaviour among persons with intellectual disabilities: Focus on experiences. *Journal of Applied Research in Intellectual Disabilities* 28(2): 61–80.

McGill, P., Bradshaw, J., Smyth, G., Hurman, M., and Roy, A. (2020) Capable environments. *Tizard Learning Disability Review* 25(3) 109–116.

Sappok, T., Zepperitz, S. and Hudson, M. (2022) *Meeting Emotional Needs in Intellectual Disability: The Developmental Approach*. Newburyport, MA: Hogrefe Publishing.

Treisman, K. (2022) *Organisational Trauma: An important context in staff support*. In Conniff, H. (Ed.) (2022) *Psychological Staff Support In Health Care: Thinking and practice*. Keighley: Sequoia Books.

Winnicott, D.W. (1985) *Deprivation and Delinquency*. London: Routledge.

Chapter 9:

A Moment in Time: Reflections On a Lifetime of Disability and Trauma Work

Valerie Sinason

How do we evaluate the conditions in which children and adults with intellectual disabilities are living? What stage in our lives are we at? Do we have more optimism at the start and in our primes than later on when we witness our ageing process? Can we view our own historical time or are we too embedded in it? My mind is filling with more questions as I get older.

We are daring to look more closely at the level of trauma in our own relatively lucky Western society in the UK. The government is also daring to look at the level of trauma more. One adult in four is considered to experience abuse in their lifetime; that's 11 million people in the UK. We see on television regularly the societal panic when two or three people have a rare physical condition, yet 11 million casualties – to say nothing of the impact on their family and friends – slips off the tongue easily (one in four). Indeed, if we add on the unwelcome news that perpetrators are made (not born) and often come from trauma themselves, the figures would be even higher. What does that say about our species? And, if the 'normal' population can be attacked in plain sight in our society, what happens to those with intellectual disabilities?

Understanding trauma in childhood

The eminent psycho-historian, Lloyd de Mause (1931–2020) memorably described the history of childhood as "a nightmare from which we have only recently begun to awaken" (1974). A focus on the needs and rights of children to have a life free from assault and hunger only began to be noticed in the West as a result of the women's movement in the 1960s. Awareness of the domestic abuse, rape and murder of women around the world highlighted the appalling plight of children.

It was Dr Henry Kempe (1985), a paediatrician from America, who first coined the term 'the battered child syndrome'. Before his work, bruised children were seen as 'clumsy' rather than physically abused. The treatment of those with intellectual disabilities comes last, lowest in the list of priorities. In times of war and peace around the world, resources for those with intellectual disabilities or multiple disabilities were the least provided. The eugenicist wish to stop all procreation of people with disabilities was actualised by death-making cultures, with physical and sexual abuse endemic (Corbett and Cottis, 2019; Wolfensberger, 1987).

It was only in 1986 that the UK, a relatively fortunate Western country, abolished assault of children by teachers in schools – four years after the European Court of Human Rights ruled on it. In the UK, it was only in 1967 that the Plowden Report advocated child-centred teaching and in 1978 that the Warnock Report recommended integration of children with learning difficulties into mainstream schools. We are all breathing in the culture and politics of our time and it takes time to see how we are embedded in it.

A focus on disability

Just one year later, in 1979, I was 33 and a trainee child psychotherapist at the Tavistock Clinic in London – the largest NHS psychotherapy teaching and treatment centre in the UK – when adult psychoanalyst Neville Symington opened a new workshop to focus specifically on disability. At that time (the golden age of the Tavistock Clinic), if you encountered a new subject that merited further research, you had the freedom to open a workshop and other colleagues had the freedom to join. Clinical research, supervision, writing papers and giving talks were all crucial ways of learning more. Just a few years later, you could not use 'your' room for pro bono work, as a room was only 'your' room if it was booked for paid work. So this workshop of Neville's represented a powerful successful moment in the clinic's growth. Unusually, a man with a mild intellectual disability had been referred to the adult department, which had not happened before. Symington was amazed at the capacity of the patient to make use of a talking therapy. He immediately opened what was then called the Subnormality Workshop and notified the whole building of this. Unusually, he invited trainees to join as well.

This had a particular resonance for me (as it also did for Dr Pat Frankish, who had a similar lived experience). My father, the late Professor SS Segal OBE, was Head of Schools for children with a disability at that time (and finally Director of Ravenswood Village, a residential community for adults with disabilities). He created the Guild of Teachers for Backward Children and the Council for Special Education, in addition to editing a journal called *Forward Trends in the Treatment of Backward Children*.

He helped to activate both the Plowden Report and the Warnock Reports, emphasising *No Child is Ineducable* (1969). This made the clarion call that children with disabilities should be in school rather than in hospital and insisted that education was failing these children, not that they were unable to make use of it.

So I was very excited by this development – although there was a psychological pause while I weighed up whether or not it was Oedipal to join the workshop. Once I had decided it would be equally Oedipal not to join, I joined and found that I was at home. The subject was like home for me! Not only had I had a lifetime of going on holiday with my father's schools for boys with intellectual disabilities, but also my maternal grandmother had a mild disability stemming from trauma. My whole life as a child psychotherapist and later as an adult psychoanalyst was transformed in this moment.

The random chances we get as children and adults, which can lead us to flourish in unexpected ways, need to be as noted as much as the vagaries of external negative factors. If Neville Symington had not started that workshop, my whole life could have followed a different path. The random gifts and curses we gain generationally and intergenerationally join with these chances and choices. When Symington and his colleagues described, as a research finding, that they found they were wearing their dullest oldest clothes when they met such patients, Dr Pat Frankish – who had her own lived experience from her parents' work – correctly asked: "Isn't that acting out the counter-transference rather than noting it?" Before it became a publicly debated issue, we were learning how much lived experience mattered and that – however junior were at the time – we had an 'at-homeness' with our clients that could not be trained for. Symington recognised and welcomed this.

In 1981, Symington published his first paper on disability and for the next few years created an atmosphere in which curiosity and theoretical exploration were welcomed. He was a genuinely democratic convenor and thinker who welcomed ideas from the newly qualified as much as from the senior consultants. As the only child psychotherapist in the workshop, I was allocated severe and profound child cases and relished the extra supervision. However, in 1985 and much to the loss of the Tavistock Clinic, Symington and his psychoanalyst wife Joan Symington emigrated to Australia.

In this initial period of the workshop, Jon Stokes and I – the two most involved members, who later took on the workshop ourselves – witnessed a familiar pattern. Drawn by the excitement and skill of Symington, other psychoanalysts took on an individual case each but then the intensity of the involvement stopped and they left the workshop. This pattern was repeated internationally as well. However, our interest and excitement grew and it was our perseverance in the subject that led to the core group of us staying in contact over the decades.

Jon Stokes (who later became chair of the adult department at the Tavistock Clinic and is now a pre-eminent leadership coach) and I – now a newly qualified child and adolescent psychotherapist (who would later become an adult psychoanalyst with a PhD on trauma and disability) – were able to grow the workshop, enhancing the contacts the Symingtons had made with Professor Joan Bicknell of St George's Hospital and her then senior registrar Dr Sheila Hollins (now Professor Sheila Baroness Hollins). We noted that those who remained in the workshop fell into clear categories:

- immigrants and foreign students who knew what it felt like to be different and/or unwanted;
- those with someone with a disability in their family; and
- those who had experienced the cruelty of upper-class boarding schools and the problems of intellectual giftedness.

Together, our families covered all those categories.

We built up the newly renamed Mental Handicap Workshop and a period of networking and theoretical creativity followed (Sinason, 1988a,b,c; Stokes and Sinason, 1992). We also noted the ubiquity of trauma in the lives of children and adults with intellectual difficulties. The fact that the workshop included child and adult practitioners allowed us to have a view of the experiences of citizens with disabilities across the age span and of the powerful impact of shame and stigma, which are societal death wishes. Membership of the workshop was free to anyone in the Tavistock Clinic and to anyone outside whom we invited. This felt the height of collegiality, sharing new ideas and research without fees being required.

Terminology: adapting and evolving

Anyone studying this area must make a note on psycholinguistics. When Neville Symington created his workshop it was called the Subnormality Workshop – the right-on word at the time. As I showed in my book *Mental Handicap and the Human Condition: New Approaches from the Tavistock* (1992), the more vulnerable the subject the more speedily the language changes. Each generation hopes that the new name they have created or endorsed will bring positive changes but it never works beyond a few years. The pain of the subject enters the new word and dismantles the language. This is the history of euphemisms. We each hope that the new word of our time will remain the 'woke' word, alive to inequality and stigma, but hubris descends.

Those struggling with the current hopes and fears about pronouns and identity would do well to look into the psycholinguistic history for euphemisms in the field of disability. One benefit of decades in the same subject is we can point the finger at ourselves for both attacking the old words and bringing in new words that become equally attacked and redundant. When Jon Stokes and I later took on the workshop, we proudly changed the name from 'Subnormality Workshop' to 'Mental Handicap Workshop'. I liked the word 'handicap' as it came from a medieval game of 'hand in the cap', in which you either got a reward or a forfeit that was placed in a hat. However, we then found a new generation angry with us and calling out for 'learning difficulty', followed by 'special needs' and now 'intellectual disability'. Then came the grammar.

While I could be an overweight woman or a tired woman, there was a new war of pronouns and adverbs. You were a woman with a learning disability or an intellectual disability, in the hope that by putting the word 'woman' first you were improving human rights. Each generation hopes that their moment in the sun will bring mutative change and, so far, each then experiences a momentary triumph – which can last a few years – followed by the hubris of being in the hot seat, equally guilty of grammatical sin, cancellation by pronouns, adverbs, and ableism. Can we bear to hold in our minds and hearts the transience of our efforts? I have watched the societal pain the debate about transitioning evokes and triggers. If only we could hold in mind that the words people fight about represent the deepest societal wounds. How I wish we could wrap words of comfort like a soft blanket around the burdened shoulders of society's minorities and outcasts.

I am writing this at the age of 78; when reflecting on the years of positive experiences we find there is still a long way to go. A seismic shift in the human rights of people with intellectual disabilities can only be tested against decades. Our small moment of triumph for our client group felt as though it was eternal but, with the passing of time and set against a historical backdrop, the failures are now far more noticeable.

A new movement

There was a group of us who together formed a movement and, between 1979 and 1988, a new peak of enthusiasm and growth came. And our own movement was nurtured by the background movements for freedom to have an abortion, to use contraception, and/or to be homosexual. The painfully named Sexual Offences Act of 1967 decriminalised consensual acts between men over 21 but this was still far from equality with the heterosexual age of consent at 16. The process of decriminalisation that began in 1967 had to wait until 2003 for gay sexuality to be entirely free from penalisation. Gay marriage was not legalised in England until 2013. If we look at the history of sexual minorities across several thousand years, we get a clearer idea of how hard it is for stigma to be removed for any group. When we consider women's bodies (ie, half the population), it was only in 1967 that abortion was legalised in this country and we can see what a powerful issue that remains.

But here we were with our Olympic steps, however long they took to be actualised. There were four key centres in England and we were all interconnected. Dr Pat Frankish and Dr Nigel Beail in 'the North' were a major early constellation, whereby – in their attempt to form a union of like-minded colleagues – they created the Yorkshire Supervision Group. They had attended the first conference created by Neville Symington and realised their long work experiences had led to deep knowledge that they could contribute.

St George's Hospital in South West London, with Professor Joan Bicknell and Dr Sheila Hollins (now Professor Sheila Baroness Hollins), was the second key centre and I worked there part-time for 16 years alongside my work at the Tavistock Clinic. Dr Georgina Parkes joined us from there. Professor Hollins' son Nigel had a mild intellectual disability and it was in looking for the best communication aids for him that Sheila and her husband Martin created Books Beyond Words, the key books for children and adults with intellectual disabilities. Nigel, now an adult, is a lead trainer and author on Books Beyond Words for other people with intellectual disabilities. St George's Hospital was the first NHS workplace to employ people with learning disabilities as lecturers.

Respond, a charity working with abuse and disability, were a key independent London group featuring Alan Corbett, Tamsin Cottis and Steve Morris. Alan and Tamsin continued the work, which was later added to by Noelle Blackman, David O'Driscoll, Richard Curen and Shanawaz al Haque.

The Tavistock Clinic with Jon Stokes and myself in North West London linked together everyone who was interested in psychoanalytic thinking and application. Our respective psychology, psychotherapy and psychiatry organisations did not, on the whole, embrace this mixture adequately and the psychoanalytic institutions were supportive but not interested enough to join.

After seven years of joint work, Jon Stokes became head of the adult department at the Tavistock Clinic and had to give up co-running the workshop. I continued solo for a few years and then invited Dr Sheila Bichard, an educational psychologist, to co-run the workshop with me. This provided the chance of multidisciplinary work and, in 1989, we renamed the workshop as the 'Mental Handicap Psychotherapy and Psychology Research Workshop'. Judith Usiskin, another child psychotherapist, joined the team and provided crucial parent work and research. Isabel Hernandes Halton, a consultant psychotherapist from the Tavistock Clinic's adult department, and Julian Lousada co-ran adult groups with me. Professor Brett Kahr ran workshops together with Jenny Sprince, Janet Bungener, Louise Emmanuel and other Tavistock Clinic members. We were able to prove conclusively that children and adults with mild, severe and profound multiple disabilities could make use of talking therapies and improve in emotional functioning, even though IQ was fixed.

The changes we were spearheading were aided by international movements. Who can tabulate the wider external historical context that enables (or disables) certain movements? The times were indeed a-changing, as Bob Dylan's song endorsed. The organisations we were grateful to at this time were the International Association for the Scientific Study of Intellectual Disability (IASSID) and the European Association for Mental Health in Intellectual Disability (MHID).

In 1988, IASSID held its major four-year conference in Dublin. Founded in the 1960s, it aimed to encourage highest-level research. It also had ethical concerns about the treatment of people with intellectual disabilities. In 1988, the UK also saw the start of the Association of Psychoanalytic Psychotherapy in the Health Service (APP). I was encouraged to create a Mental Handicap Section for it and we added our European colleagues to this as well as to the Tavistock Clinic workshops.

Johan de Groeuf, a leading psychoanalyst from Belgium, was the key addition, as he assiduously connected key Europeans to our small number, including Christian Gaedt, Evelyn Heinemann and Dietmut Niedecken from Germany, Claude Boulobza, Simone Korf Sausse (herself part of a major French network), Annie Stammler, Colette M Assouly-Piquet, Cecile Herrou, Claire Morelle, Monique Schneider and Regine Scelles from France, and Joost Demuynck from Belgium. I also met with Maria Eugenia Cid Rodriguez from Spain, Yvonne Gilljam from Sweden, Wai Jung Lee and Arnold Wellman from Canada, and Richard Ruth et al from the USA.

The first three psychotherapy centres for people with disabilities in Scandinavia were established as a result of our international links and perhaps the most important contact outside Europe was with Professor Leslie Swartz at the Cape Town Child Guidance Clinic (and now at Stellanbosch), to which I became a yearly visitor with an honorary consultant psychotherapist post at the Child Guidance Clinic. As well as Leslie Swartz, key links were with Professor Brian Watermeyer, Professor Sally Swartz and Dr Bev Dickman, who trained prosecutors to work with adults with disabilities who disclosed rape.

Our ten-week courses proliferated and our new one-year course became successful. It was a glorious decade for us. We were able to prove the obvious – ie, that people with all levels of disability could make use of a talking treatment, could improve their quality of life, and were able to find ways of expressing their traumatic experiences.

International talks and trainings followed. In 1990, PAOS invited several of us to speak in the Netherlands and Garry Prouty presented his pre-therapy process, especially designed for people with intellectual disabilities. Dosen and Menoloscino (1990) published the first book on the treatment of depression in people with disabilities. The People First self-advocacy movement came from the USA to the UK. The concept of normalisation was developed in Denmark and Sweden by Bank-Mikkelson and Bengt Nirje and taken up in the USA by the President's Committee on Mental Retardation. Within the UK, the Bowlby Centre highlighted the need for therapy for people with intellectual disabilities.

The international organisations were largely male-dominated and psychiatric at that period, so the impact of Professor Joan Bicknell, Professor Sheila Baroness Hollins and Dr Pat Frankish made a significant difference. Indeed, Dr Pat Frankish and Professor Sheila Baroness Hollins became President of the British Psychological Society and President of the Royal College of Psychiatry, respectively.

For the next decade, my colleagues and I had reached a period of happiness and excitement in our work. Together with Dr Pat Frankish, Professor Sheila Baroness Hollins, Dr Nigel Beail and the Respond team and our other key colleagues, we were able to show that children and adults with intellectual disabilities were not only wrongly excluded from talking therapies but were also able to make major emotional change through accessing psychotherapy. The first edition of my book, *Mental Handicap and the Human Condition: New Approaches from the Tavistock*, was published by Free Association Books in 1992, when I was 46.

A lifetime commitment was what we all gave to this work and each assessment and treatment added to our shared knowledge. In 1996, when de Groeuf brought us all together for a three-day conference, we were thrilled to receive a message from the French genius Maude Mannoni.

In 2000, that same group of us were inspired by leading psychoanalytic psychotherapist and historian Professor Brett Kahr to found the Institute of

Psychotherapy and Disability (IPD) – under the aegis of which, we could all connect independently from our other accrediting organisations. This was a normal 20-year trajectory for a career. However, gradually, something else was seeded that was to change the sense of slow-growing success.

Ten years earlier, in 1989, a group of us was rocked by a new awareness of sexual trauma. I had been working with children and adults with intellectual disabilities for ten years then, finding a level of abuse that was far higher than within the general population. Dr Pat Frankish, Respond, St George's Hospital and others then sadly became aware that our client group not only had to deal with the difficulties of a disability but also all the negative trauma-loaded ways they were treated. Leading child abuse prevention pioneer Dr Arnon Bentovim confirmed that the rates for disability and abuse were higher than for other minority groups. Inevitably, this made disability therapy pioneers into abuse prevention pioneers, too.

A Swedish psychologist, Anders Svensson, sought help from me for his treatment of a woman with an intellectual disability in Sweden who disclosed narratives of ritual abuse. It was a level of abuse that traumatised me, as I had never heard of such torture before outside war. It took months before I could speak about it (Sinason, 1992). After mentioning it in one sentence during a conference on child abuse in Scotland, I was suddenly overwhelmed with phone calls at the Tavistock Clinic from women mainly, alleging ritual abuse. These women were mostly white, middle-class and highly intelligent.

Foundations of the Clinic for Dissociative Studies

I could not leave them unheard and gained Department of Health funding for research to be carried out at the Tavistock and Portman NHS Foundation Trust. The nature of the disclosures shocked even hardened forensic psychotherapists and, when the grant ended, the Tavistock Clinic was glad to finish the research by passing it on to me to work on privately. The disability work that had brought great acclaim to the Tavistock Clinic was now in danger of being soured. We met with 51 courageous individuals and were shocked by the police's lack of power to listen and follow through. We were pleased to show that the narratives were not scripts from fundamentalist groups and churches and that there was no mental health reason to cast doubt on their narratives. We also found to our shock that a significant minority of our group had Dissociative Identity Disorder, the new term for Multiple Personality Disorder – a subject we had not been trained in.

So, after a few years of Department of Health funding to research the nature of ritual abuse disclosures following support of the treatment of a Swedish woman with an intellectual disability, the subject rocked British society. Up until this moment, there had been a curious acceptance that children and adults with intellectual disabilities had been abused. However, in this forerunner to the #MeToo movement, there was a moment when the capacity of the country to take on more was stymied.

I had created a workshop to study the subject, made international links, and undertaken research. In other words, I had followed the time-honoured Tavistock approach when faced with a new subject. However, social pressures had already changed. The ongoing realisation of abuse rings, of abuse by VIPs, and of abuse in homes for people with intellectual disabilities had caused compassion fatigue and splits in society. Ritual abuse – the use of ritual as a way of terrifying children and adults – was clearly too much. Perhaps there is only a certain amount of reality any population can bear in one historical period.

In 1998, after the Tavistock Clinic had thankfully included disability therapy as part of its patient group instead of relying on the pro bono work augmented by small research grants that I had managed on, I felt free to leave the Tavistock Clinic and create the Clinic for Dissociative Studies, aided by Dr Arnon Bentovim, Dr Phil Mollon, Professor Howard Steele (who provided the psychiatric, psychological and attachment assessments) and Professor John Morton (who provided memory research), as well as by former Detective Chief Inspector Clive Driscoll in an historic agreement with the Metropolitan Police. I retired at 70. The Clinic for Dissociative Studies is still flourishing, has just had its 25th anniversary, and attachment-based psychotherapist and former chair of the Bowlby Centre Mark Linington is CEO. It was no surprise to me that core colleagues in the field of intellectual disability recognised the reality of organised ritual abuse and DID.

Indeed, Dr Pat Frankish (2022) wrote a book on the subject with young people with lived experience. It is also important to note that, when my edited book *Treating Survivors of Satanist Abuse* was published in 1992, it included chapters from Professor Joan Bicknell, Dr Nigel Beail, Dr Alan Corbett, Professor Brett Kahr and Professor Judith Trowell.

Institute of Psychotherapy and Disability

At the time of writing and at the age of 78, I am proud to be President of the IPD, which connects a core group of us. We felt hopeful and excited when we created the IPD in 2000. Although our work came from the power of the therapeutic encounter and involved small numbers, we understood the major applications that were possible. By focusing on assessment processes that could be therapeutic in their own right, Dr Pat Frankish was making her public statement and, by teaching and theorising on secondary mental handicap and opportunist handicap, I was spreading psychoanalytic knowledge. With several of us – Professor Sheila Baroness Hollins, Dr Pat Frankish, Dr Roger Banks and I – now past retirement age, with the sad premature death of Dr Alan Corbett, and with middle generation (Dr Georgina Parkes and Dr Angelina Veiga) overworked, what have we achieved and how do we evaluate it?

We are about to produce our first IPD book for Routledge, *Disability Therapy: What It Is and Why It Matters*, which has taken several years to produce. It was the brainchild of Dr Alan Corbett, a luminous colleague, and passed through several co-editors due to COVID-19 and various life events before ending up with Dr Angelina Veiga and I. The time it has taken has evoked much reflection. Despite our love and passion for the work, we felt we were carrying a baby with a disability and that everything took longer. Our highly qualified pioneering members have hardly enlarged during this period. Austerity, cuts, stigma, shame, pain and trauma join together to embattle the subject. And the subject includes all the pain of the world located in our precious citizens, which they carry with such fortitude.

When I had the privilege of meeting the brave therapists working in Leros and saw the terrible conditions in which citizens with intellectual disabilities had been kept, Dr John Tsiantis arranged for me to go to one of the worst wards. A group of named men – chained together to avoid falling out of bed – moved so that one of them, a man with Down syndrome, could look up and offer his hand when I said I was Valerie Sinason from England. I shook his hand. Then I slowly walked out of that terrifying cold hall to scrub my hands.

A year later, I went to see the first group home in Athens. The man I had met before opened the door with a beaming smile, dressed smartly. With an interpreter following, he showed me his room and a wardrobe with two pairs of trousers and shirts. In the therapy group, he said to me: "I remember you. You held my hand in Leros."

There is a 'Leros' in every country. An *oubliette*. A place where the denials, disavowal, and compassion fatigue of a country join together to deprive groups who trigger the hurtlines in society. Together with our joy, our political work and our clinical work, perhaps we have to accept that some groups will never receive a total welcome and proper enabling in our lifetime. This does not stop our reaching out or our 'in-touchness'. Nor does it stop the wonderful daily miracles we witness when enabled fellow citizens tell us who they are. But against those eternal moments of change are the abysses of hurt people and countries hurting others.

To end at the beginning. Most parents hope that their child will have the best of their genetic inheritance. In the West, most parents feel that they are charge of procreation, not that nature is involved. To have a baby that has turned out 'wrong' is seen as a personal shame. The outside world is failing in not offering a warm welcome to the new baby. What does therapy do? One mother said: "It is not going to make him normal, so what is the point?" Do other professionals have this view unconsciously too and see those of us doing this work as gullible and naïve? Against that, we have the beauty of the communications we have received. And love is timeless.

Meanwhile, we give thanks to pioneers like Pat who provide 24-hour homes and culture and community, recognition of identity, and the beginnings of safety.

References

Corbett, A. (2019) *Intellectual Disability and Psychotherapy: The theories, practice and influence of Valerie Sinason*. London: Routledge.

DeMause, L. (1974) *The History of Western Childhood*. New York: Harper and Row.

Dosen, A. and Menolascino, F. (1990) *Depression in Mentally Retarded Children and Adults*. Amsterdam, Leiden: Logon Publications.

Frankish, P. (2016) *Disability Psychotherapy: An innovative approach to trauma-informed care*. London: Karnac.

Frankish, P. (2022) *Trauma and Dissociation*. Shoreham: Pavilion Publishing.

Kempe, C.H., Silverman, F.N., *et al.* (1985) The battered-child syndrome. *Child Abuse And Neglect* **9**: 143–154.

Segal, S.S. (1969) *No Child is Ineducable*. Oxford: Pergamon Press.

Sinason, V. (1986) Secondary Mental Handicap and Its Relationship to Trauma. *Psychoanalytic Psychotherapy* **2**(2): 131–154.

Sinason, V. (1988) Dolls and Bears; from symbolic equalition to symbol. The use of different play material for sexually abused children, *Brit.J of Psychotherapy* **4** (4) 350-63

Sinason, V. (1988) Smiling, swallowing, sickening and stupefying. *Psychoanalytic Psychotherapy* **3**(2) 97–111.

Sinason, V. (1988) Richard III, Hephaestrus and Echo: Sexuality and mental/multiple handicap. *Journal of Child Psychotherapy* **5**(2): 251.

Sinason, V. (1989) *Barry: A Case Study* in Brechin, A. and Walmsley, T. (Eds.) Making a Connection. Milton Keynes: Open University Press.

Stokes, J.B. and Sinason, V. (1992) *Secondary Mental Handicap as a Defence in Waitman*, A. and Conboy-Hill, S. (Eds.) (1992) *Psychotherapy and Mental Handicap*. London: Sage. pp.46–58.

Symington, N. (1981) The psychotherapy of a subnormal patient. *British Journal of Psychology* **54**:187–199.

Wolfensberger, W. (1987) The New Genocide of Handicapped and Afflicted People. Syracuse: Syracuse University Division of Special Education and Rehabilitation.

Chapter 10:

The Development of Psychotherapy for People Who Have Intellectual Disabilities: A Personal Journey

Professor Nigel Beail

In this chapter, I want to tell the story of how I and others began providing psychotherapy to people who have intellectual disabilities. My interest in psychotherapy began when I studied A-level psychology and continued when I studied for a degree in psychology. However, I did not consider clinical psychology as a career, owing to my interest in research. It was while undertaking a PhD that I started attending meetings of the Psychology and Psychotherapy Association and then started training in personal construct psychotherapy. It was one of my supervisors who suggested that I might pursue clinical psychology, as she did not think I was cut out for a career in academia. So, on completion of my PhD, I embarked on clinical psychology training.

After qualifying as a clinical psychologist in 1984, I took a post in a community team for people with intellectual disabilities. At that time, most clinical psychologists who supported people with intellectual disabilities worked in the behavioural tradition; however, during my training, I became concerned at the lack of alternative approaches being made available. While most of my training had focused on behavioural ways of working, we were also taught about person-centred and psychodynamic psychotherapy. I was fortunate to have a placement with a psychologist who was psychodynamically trained and who encouraged me to attend her supervision group with a psychoanalyst. Before I qualified as a clinical psychologist, I had developed a passion for working with people with intellectual disabilities and expanding the therapeutic offer made to them.

Psychotherapy and people with intellectual disabilities before 1980

Prior to the 1980s, psychodynamic practitioners' views on working with people with intellectual disabilities were negative. This may be rooted in a statement made by Sigmund Freud in 1904: "Patients who do not possess a reasonable degree of education and reliable character should be refused." For Freud, "the qualification that is the determining factor of fitness for psychoanalytic treatment is whether the patient is educable". Freud's statement seems to have had a significant impact on selection and exclusion criteria for psychotherapeutic treatment for almost a century (Bender, 1993). By way of example, Rogers and Dyamond (1954) stated that person-centred psychotherapy was not suitable for people with intellectual disabilities because it requires insight, verbal communication, and other elements inherent in normal intelligence. Psychoanalysts Tyson and Sandler (1971) stated that mental deficiency is a contraindication for psychoanalysis. Indeed, being of average intelligence became an attribute for suitability for counselling and psychotherapy (Bloch, 1979; Brown and Pedder, 1979).

Other than literature on exclusion criteria, the literature concerning psychodynamic therapy with people with intellectual disabilities was extremely limited, as was any information on its history. O'Driscol (2009) and Sinason (1992) tried to map the early history but unfortunately earlier published accounts of psychodynamic psychotherapy with people with intellectual disabilities have been ambiguous as to the nature or degree of impairment presented by clients and further confused by a lack of consensus, consistency and clarity in the terminology used to describe people with intellectual disabilities and the nature of their impairments (Sinason, 1992). As Sinason (1992) concluded, the history is painfully short and where efforts were made these were poorly documented.

During my clinical training in the 1980s, a debate was taking place within the pages of the *Bulletin of the British Psychological Society* about the suitability of people with intellectual disabilities for psychotherapy following a symposium on psychotherapy and people with intellectual disabilities presented at a British Psychological Society Conference at the end of 1981. This initial criticism concerned the use of the term 'subnormal' by the symposiasts. But then, in a letter to the *Bulletin*, Church (1982) argued that "such therapy would produce as much a useful result as an engineer using a watch-maker's tool to build a bridge". He questioned the symposiasts' claim that psychodynamic psychotherapy was 'highly promising' for people with intellectual disabilities.

In response, Cullen (1982) pointed out that people with intellectual disabilities are not a homogeneous group and that if a prerequisite for engaging in psychodynamic therapy is the ability to converse in some way with the therapist, then there is no reason why a very large number of people with intellectual disabilities should not enjoy the benefits of such therapy.

The negative views held from Freud onwards did not resonate with my placement experience in a long-stay hospital for people with intellectual disabilities. However, negative views continued and were summarised in a paper by Bender (1993) on the history of therapeutic disdain towards people with intellectual disabilities. Critical views persisted into the new millennium – for example, Sturmey (2005) published a paper entitled *Against Psychotherapy for People Who Have Mental Retardation*.

Emerging ideas

A clinical psychology placement working with people with intellectual disabilities was a core part of clinical psychology training. My placement was in an NHS hospital that was home to 440 children and adults who had intellectual disabilities. My supervisor was aware of my interest and training in psychotherapy and suggested I apply my skills with some of the patients in the hospital who she felt would benefit from this approach. My experience during my placement of engaging people with intellectual disabilities in psychotherapy was positive.

My next placement was with older adults and adults with neuropsychological problems. My supervisor was a clinical psychologist who worked psychodynamically with older people. So, I began to learn how to work psychodynamically and attended weekly supervision with a psychoanalyst.

What I learned on these placements was that there seemed to be no reason why most people with intellectual disabiliies could not engage in psychodynamic psychotherapy. I therefore wrote a short piece for the Division of Clinical Psychology's newsletter, making the case for psychotherapy for people with intellectual disabilities (Beail, 1985).

Part of my psychodynamic supervision involved using the ideas of David Malan (1979) in formulating clients' problems. The psychodynamic ideas I was exposed to at this time were based on Freud's theories – although we also had lectures on Melanie Klein and I learned about attachment theory and object relations theory.

When I was coming to the end of my training, the move from hospital to community care was gaining momentum and the government were funding more posts for clinical psychologists in community teams for people with intellectual disabilities. I applied for and was offered a post in such a team. I wanted to use this opportunity to develop the provision of psychotherapy. From my first day, it was clear that there were more than enough referrals of people with intellectual disabilities in need of psychological help. I then found a suitable room in which to work.

What intrigued me was that my referrals were of people who had the same mental health needs as seen in general adult mental health services, yet the request was for me to offer behaviour modification. My experience of behaviour modification was of its application in hospital wards where there was a degree of control over the variable that caused and maintained behaviour. This did not transfer to community settings. In response, I assessed my patients' needs and – where appropriate – offered individual psychotherapy.

The main challenge I faced was obtaining clinical supervision for working psychodynamically. The psychoanalyst from whom I was receiving supervision declined, stating it was outside of his boundaries. I therefore contacted other psychologist in the wider area and this led to the formation of group of clinical psychologists who were endeavouring to work psychotherapeutically with people with intellectual disabilities. After the group was formed, Dr Pat Frankish wrote letters to the journals of the

British Psychological Society and British Institute for Learning Disabilities, seeking to form links with others working psychotherapeutically with people with intellectual disabilities. Pat was living within a reasonable distance from where the group met so we invited her to join our group, which she did. Dr Valerie Sinason, who was then based at the Tavistock Clinic in London, also responded to Pat's letter and so links were forged with her. At that time, Valerie had taken over the Mental Handicap Workshop at the Tavistock Clinic in London. This had been started by Neville Symington and Jon Stokes, who were two of the symposiasts at the British Psychological Society Conference.

The new group in Yorkshire became a co-supervision group but also allowed for some personal therapy for group members. The group kept its activities quiet, as there was some hostility towards psychodynamic practice from other psychologists. Our link with Dr Valerie Sinason was productive. Valerie obtained funding form the Child Psychotherapy Trust to come to Yorkshire weekly to provide the Tavistock Clinic's course on psychotherapy for people with intellectual disabilities. As the funding was generous, we decided to open this course to others in our profession and it was very well attended. The supervision group also grew as the original members started to provide supervision to trainees and other clinical psychologists.

As our confidence increased, we became more open and started to present at conferences and provide training to clinical psychologists. We then formed the Association for Psychotherapy for People with Intellectual Disabilities and put on our own conferences. Pat Frankish and Valerie Sinason also began attending and presenting at international conferences such as those of the International Association for the Scientific Study of Intellectual Disabilities and the European Association for Mental Health Intellectual Disability. I then joined them in this endeavour.

Learning to adapt psychotherapy

As clinical psychologists, we had learned to adapt our therapeutic approach to work with children and so we saw no issue in adapting our approach to working with adults with intellectual disabilities. NICE (2016) now recommends adapting therapies according to each individual, including preferences, level of understanding, and strengths and needs, while considering other aspects of disability such as physical, sensory and communication needs.

As I work in the NHS, I take a time-limited approach and thus need to maintain a therapeutic focus as opposed to the free association used in longer-term approaches such as psychoanalysis. We have found that, in terms of practical arrangements, it is helpful for people with intellectual disabilities to have appointments at the same time and place each week. Some flexibility may also be needed around session length, as not all can tolerate 50 minutes. People with intellectual disabilities may need longer to tell the therapist about their problem. The therapist needs to take account of the client's developmental level and communication ability and adapt their approach accordingly. So, we need to keep language simple, using the language of the client. As a rule, we use short sentences and words up to a maximum of three syllables.

Sometimes people with intellectual disabilities struggle to find the words to communicate their distress. This does not mean that they are not aware of it. They may have a good visual representation of their distress, but not the vocabulary to describe it in the session. The therapist asks the client describe or show them what is distressing them, but this can be aided by offering possible labels for objects, feelings, and behaviours. The client may also struggle to recall the order in which events in their life occurred. When this is the case, the therapist can help by suggesting that the client draw a visual representation of things they can recall and then work to try and build their chronology through exploration in therapy. Some clients also find it helpful to use objects to communicate in sessions.

The emergence of new literature

One distinct problem we had in the early days of providing psychodynamic psychotherapy was the lack of published literature on its use with people with intellectual disabilities. It is generally accepted that the first case study concerning psychodynamic psychotherapy for a person with intellectual disabilities was published in 1981 (Symington, 1981). Neville Symington reported his therapeutic work with 'Harry Smith' (a pseudonym), who was 33 years old and had an IQ of 59. Prior to therapy starting, he met with Harry's parents and with the staff at Harry's place of work to gather more information and 'assess the situation'. This is something that some clients prefer when they attend for assessment.

Symington provided Harry with a one-to-one relationship, meeting once each week at his (Symington's) place of work for two years. Symington did not use a couch but, rather, two chairs. He remained seated but Harry often moved around the room. I tried offering a couch to my clients but, like Symington, found my clients would sit up, get off and walk around and then find a chair to sit on. Symington depicts himself being non-directive, not directly answering Harry's questions, and ascribing possible meaning to Harry's behaviour, dialogue, and way of relating to him – a process he described as interpretation. He also describes himself using gestures and metaphor to convey concepts to Harry.

Symington (1981) describes himself attempting to understand the meaning behind the information he gathers in the sessions. However, Symington did not describe the process of how he came to understand these meanings. He clearly describes the communication of his interpretations but does not inform us of the process through which they were developed. A core competence of a clinical psychologist is formulation, so I felt the need to do something about this.

To begin with, I recorded some sessions with some of my patients. This was frowned upon by psychotherapists at the time, who felt it interfered with the therapeutic process. However, it enabled me to write illustrative accounts of the therapeutic process with two men with intellectual disabilities. My aim was to illustrate the process through showing the three main actions of the therapist: clarification, confrontation, and interpretation (Sublette and Novick, 2004). Dr Pat Frankish and I used one of these case studies to illustrate to others how we work through role-play. Pat and I were then invited to contribute to an edited book on therapeutic approaches to working with people with intellectual disabilities, whereby I published my case studies illustrating the process (Beail, 1989). Concurrently, others were also publishing case studies, followed by the first case series (Frankish, 1989).

In 1992, Dr Valerie Sinason published *Mental Handicap and the Human Condition: Approaches from the Tavistock*. This contained several theoretical advances grounded in her clinical work – in particular, her observations on forms of secondary handicap being used as a defence against trauma. Notably, by this time, Dr Pat Frankish, Dr Valerie Sinason and I were all documenting the role of trauma in the lives of the patients we were seeing (see Beail (2021)). However, in the 1980s and early 1990s, this was not so widely accepted as a factor in psychological distress. Nonetheless, several strands of clinical and social work started to come together, and the physical and sexual abuse of children became an acknowledged problem. Even so, it took a while before it became accepted that people with intellectual disabilities are at risk of abuse.

Following disclosures of abuse made during therapy sessions, my colleague Dr Sharon Warden and I became concerned and decided to undertake an audit of the frequency of sexual abuse in a cohort of outpatients. We found that 25% of our patients had, during therapy, disclosed sexual abuse. We also linked this to the distress they presented with, owing to the way the abuse emerged during therapy (Beail and Warden, 1995). We also observed, as Sigmund Freud and Melanie Klein had done, that adults with intellectual disabilities acted out their distress both in sessions and outside therapy (Beail, 2021). Acting out is considered a contraindication for psychodynamic treatment, but we accepted this as the person's way of communicating their distress (Brown and Pedder, 1979). So, we had to develop psychotherapeutic ways to contain this and work it through (see Beail and Newman (2005) and Sinason (1992)).

Developing practice

My therapeutic work with people with intellectual disabilities evolved from the Freudian model (Freud, 1940) I had been introduced to during my training to being more influenced by the work and ideas of child psychoanalysts such as Melanie Klein, Donald Winnicott and John Bowlby. Dr Pat Frankish also introduced me to the work of Margaret Mahler, which has greatly influenced her work (Frankish, 2016). I have also gone back to Freud's early trauma theory (Freud, 1896), which he unfortunately struggled to embrace throughout his life, but never quite abandoned altogether (Beail, 2021).

It became clear that working with people who are developmentally delayed can be informed by the work and findings of those who work with typically developing children, as there is often a developmental equivalence. However, there is also difference in that developmentally delayed adults often present as dyssynchronous across their physical, social, cognitive, and emotional development. However, while finding theories from child psychotherapy informative, I continued to be informed by the approach of David Malan in my formulation of clients' problems.

The literature was emerging on psychodynamic psychotherapy and people with intellectual disabilities, offering different insights and perspectives (De Groef and Heineman, 1999; Simpson and Miller, 2004); however, regarding the formulation of clients' problems, the issues I found with Symington's case study persisted. In 2013, Tom Jackson and I published a review paper on the practice of psychodynamic psychotherapy with people with intellectual disabilities (Jackson and Beail, 2013). We found that we were the only practitioners describing how we developed our formulations.

Formulating hypotheses in psychodynamic psychotherapy: the contribution of Malan

The aim of psychodynamic psychotherapy is to work with the client to form hypotheses about their problematic experience, which we can then put to the client. This is usually referred to as interpretation. The aim of interpretation is to help the client become aware of something of which they were not previously conscious. Here, I describe Malan's model and approach as depicted in the form of two triangles (see Figure 1).

Figure 10.1: Malan's triangles

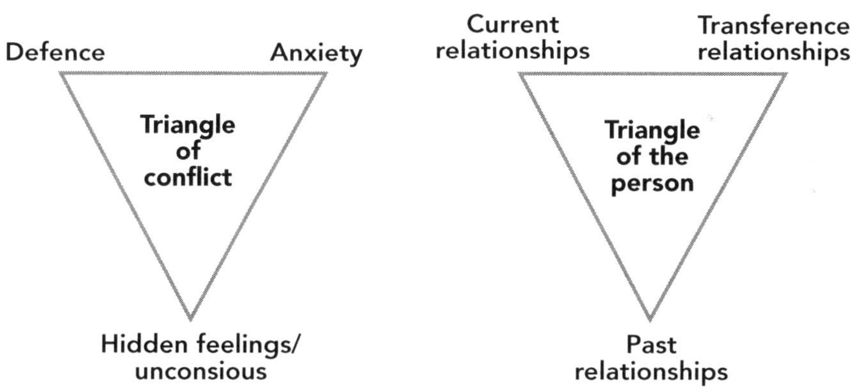

The Triangle of Conflict contains unconscious memories and impulses (Hidden Feelings), emotional experience (Anxiety), and the way the person prevents these from becoming conscious (Defence). This is an interpersonal or relational approach and so attempts to help the person understand how the difficulties in the Triangle of Conflict are being perpetuated through the use of the Triangle of the Person. In the Triangle of the Person, the three corners represent the person's past relationships and attachments (Past Relationships), as well as interpersonal styles as represented in their day-to-day life (Current Relationships) and in the relationship with the therapist (Transference Relationship). In the therapeutic session, the therapist is concerned with the defences the person employs to deal with feelings (anxiety) caused by what is being defended against.

The Triangle of the Person enables the therapist to consider and try to understand the developmental factors that influence a person's experience of themselves and others from their earliest relationships onwards. One corner of the Triangle of the Person is labelled 'Transference'; this corner represents what happens in the session with the therapist. Transference was described by Freud (1912) as occurring when psychological experiences are revived and, instead of being in the past, are applied to dealings with a person in the present. Basically, the client unconsciously interacts with the therapist as they would with another or others in their current life or their past.

Further, the client's world (their experiences past and present) can be transferred into the therapeutic relationship. Thus, the client does not engage in unique behaviours with the therapist but applies what they have experienced and learned through past relationships in order to make sense of this new situation. The therapist will observe previously formed ways of relating to this new situation.

As people enter therapy owing to problematic experiences in their relationships, these patterns re-emerge in the relationship with the therapist. Thus, current and past relationship patterns become reactivated and replayed as the problematic experiences the person brings to therapy are explored. It is the through the Triangle of the Person that the therapist helps the client explore how past issues in relationships can often become a feature of current relationships and then in the relationship with the therapist.

The therapist begins by seeking information about the client's problem and then follows up with exploratory questions about what the client may be hinting at through words or behaviour or seems to be avoiding. As the therapist explores the problem with the client, they observe the client's anxiety and their attempts to reduce this by the use of defence mechanisms such as denial and projection. The aim of the therapeutic endeavour is to reach beneath the defence and anxiety to the true and hidden feeling.

At this point, the therapist can begin to trace back what is being hidden from the present transference location (the therapy room) to its origin in the past, usually to the relationship with parents or significant carers. For Malan (1979), "the importance of these two triangles is that between them they can be used to represent almost every intervention that a therapist makes and that much of the therapist's skill consists of knowing which parts of which triangle to include in his interpretation at any given moment".

So, the therapist works with the client to populate the corners of the Triangle of Conflict as it emerges in the session. The therapist draws the client's attention to the emerging feelings of anxiety and their attempts to reduce this anxiety through their defence mechanisms. The therapist can then explore the client's feelings of anxiety outside the session, as well as the client's use of their defences in relation to others, and then explore how these developed over time. The process leads to the uncovering of the hidden feelings usually located in the past – albeit sometimes in the not-too-distant past.

Malan's model can be applied to most psychodynamic theories. So, if we look at the work of Melanie Klein (1932), she identified that her child clients presented with anxieties that she described as paranoid and depressive and that they used defences such as splitting (viewing things as either one extreme or the other) and omnipotence (viewing themselves as superior) in their session with her. So, she described anxieties and defences as though they would form parts of the Triangle of Conflict that were related to unconscious or hidden experience. The anxieties and defences manifest in the transference situation with the therapist and can be explored in relation to the relationship with the therapist and current and past relationships.

In work with adults with intellectual disabilities, similar anxieties and defences have been observed. By way of example, the dependence adults with intellectual disabilities have on others to meet their day-to-day needs may lead to fear of the loss of that person or fear of abandonment due to having angry feelings towards those on whom they are dependent (depressive anxiety) and to use of defences such as omnipotence to ward this off. This may manifest in the relationship with the therapist as telling them that they don't need them and their therapy and then, outside therapy, telling their carers that they do not need them. Similarly, Dr Valerie Sinason has described defences that have manifested in sessions with adults with intellectual disabilities – notably, secondary handicaps such as the "handicapped smile" and the exaggeration of disability to keep the therapist and others at bay.

Malan's model can also guide our work in a trauma-informed way. Freud (1896) linked traumatic experiences to the development of psychological distress and mental health problems (Beail, 2021). The traumas Freud referred to at the time included sexual and physical abuse. He described his psychoanalytic method as leading the patient's attention back from their presenting problem or symptom as experienced in current relationships with others (Current Relationships in the Triangle of the Person) to the scene of significant traumatic force through which the symptom arose in the past (Past Relationships in the Triangle of the Person). Freud argued that these traumatic experiences were thrust out of conscious thought into the unconscious (Hidden Feelings in the Triangle of Conflict) through the action of a defence mechanism (Defence in the Triangle of Conflict). Freud described how people who present with psychological distress do so because a present-day event (Current Relationships in the Triangle of the Person) causes the past traumatic experiences to come into operation in the form of unconscious memories. It is the presence of these unconscious memories that give rise to the symptoms of psychological distress (Anxiety in the Triangle of Conflict).

The therapist helps the client to see the significance of a connecting link in the chain of associations from the here and now (transference) to their current distress to earlier (past) scenes of greater traumatic force. The aim is to enable the client to bring the hidden into consciousness in a safe and contained way so that these can be worked through. Ultimately, the goal of therapy is achieved as the client moves towards living with the traumatic memories in a less damaging or dysfunctional way.

Research on effectiveness and evaluating outcomes

Since I started providing psychodynamic psychotherapy in my clinical practice, I have continued to use my research skills to evaluate my work. I started evaluating outcomes on a case-by-case basis and these accumulated over time to provide case reports and case series. Then Dr Sharon Warden and I started a study of the effectiveness of psychodynamic psychotherapy with people with intellectual disabilities in routine practice, using established psychotherapy outcome measures. This was followed by working with David Newman on the assimilation of problematic experience during psychotherapy in people with intellectual disabilities. These studies are now summarised with others in a systematic review (Shepheard and Beail, 2017) and show that psychodynamic psychotherapy is an effective treatment – sadly, however, more rigorous studies including control groups have not been feasible in routine clinical practice.

I have also worked with my colleagues to evaluate the psychotherapy measures we have used with people with intellectual disabilities (see Vlissides *et al* (2016) for a review). Owing to some concerns about using outcome measures developed for the typically developing population, we went on to develop a measure of psychological distress and well-being specifically for use with people with intellectual disabilities (Vlissides, 2017). This has been used in several studies evaluating the outcome of psychotherapy with people with intellectual disabilities (Beail, 2024). The measure has now gone through further validation and a revision of this will be available soon.

Conclusion

My aim here has been to provide a brief history of how psychotherapy began to be offered to people with intellectual disabilities from around 1980 and the direction I took developing this. A range of psychodynamic theories has informed my clinical work, yet I have found that David Malan's approach to formulation works with them all. Malan developed his approach through his clinical work with typically developing adults, but the approach equally applies to adults with intellectual disabilities.

Our work with people with intellectual disabilities has confirmed that, like everyone else, they experience anxiety in response to difficulties in their life and use defence mechanisms to help them cope. I have taught this approach to many trainee clinical psychologists, psychiatrists and psychotherapists and have used this approach in published case reports and textbooks. Concurrently, I have evaluated my work through studies in my routine practice and these studies have proved useful to others wanting to develop the provision of psychotherapy. I initially worked with others to establish psychodynamic psychotherapy, then reports on cognitive behavioural psychotherapy began to appear. Encouragingly, the range of psychological therapies on offer to people with intellectual disabilities has now expanded and a full range of them is being provided (see Beail, 2016).

References

Beail, N. (1985) Psychotherapy with mentally handicapped people. *Division of Clinical Psychology Newsletter* 43: 58–59.

Beail N (1989) *Understanding Emotions: The Kleinian approach explained* in D. Brandon, D. (Ed.) (1989) *Mutual Respect: Therapeutic approaches to working with people with learning difficulties.* Surrey: Good Impression.

Beail, N. (2016). *Psychological Therapies and People Who Have Intellectual Disabilities*. Leicester: British Psychological Society.

Beail, N. (2021). Trauma-Informed Psychodynamic Psychotherapy in Beail, N., Frankish, P. and Skelly, A. (Eds.). (2021) Trauma and Intellectual Disability: Recognition, Identification, and Intervention. Shoreham: Pavilion Publishing.

Beail, N. (2021). Freud, Psychoanalysis, and Trauma: Significance in the Acknowledgement and Identification of Trauma in the Lives of People Who Have Intellectual Disabilities in Beail, N., Frankish, P. and Skelly, A. (Eds.). (2021) Trauma and Intellectual Disability: Recognition, Identification, and Intervention. Shoreham: Pavilion Publishing.

Beail, N., Kerry, E., Rawlings, G.H., and Vlissides, N. (2023). Psychological therapies outcome scale for people who have intellectual disabilities. FPID Bulletin: The Bulletin of the Faculty for People with Intellectual Disabilities 21(3): 64–65. https://doi.org/10.53841/bpsfpid.2023.21.3.64

Beail, N. and Newman, D. (2005) Psychodynamic counselling and psychotherapy for mood disorders in Sturmey, P. (Ed) (2005) Mood Disorders in People with Mental Retardation. Kingston, NY: NADD Press.

Beail, N. and Warden, S. (1995). Sexual abuse of adults with learning disabilities. Journal of Intellectual Disability Research 39: 382–387.

Bender, M. (1993). The unoffered chair: The history of therapeutic disdain towards people with a learning difficulty. Clinical Psychology Forum 54: 7–12.

Bloch, S. (1979). Assessment of patients for psychotherapy. *British Journal of Psychiatry* 135: 193–208.

Brown, D. and Pedder, J. (1979) *Introduction to Psychotherapy*. London: Methuen.

Church, M. (1982). Letter. *Bulletin of the British Psychological Society* 35: 393.

Cullen, C. (1982). Letter. *Bulletin of the British Psychological Society* 35: 470.

De Groef, J. and Heinemann, E. (1999) *Psychoanalysis and Mental Handicap.* London: Free Association Books.

Frankish, P. (1989). Meeting the emotional needs of handicapped people: a psychodynamic approach, *Journal of Mental Deficiency research.* 33: 407-14

Frankish, P. (2016) *Disability Psychotherapy: An Innovative Approach to Trauma Informed Care.* London: Karnac.

Freud, S. (1896) The aetiology of hysteria. *The Standard Edition of the Complete Psychological Works of Sigmund Freud.* London: Hogarth

Freud, S. (1904). Loewenfeld, Freud's psycho-analytic procedure. The Standard Edition of the Complete Psychological Works of Sigmund Freud. London: Hogarth.

Freud S (1912) The dynamics of transference. *The Standard Edition of the Complete Psychological Works of Sigmund Freud.* London: Hogarth.

Freud, S. (1940) An outline of psychoanalysis. *The Standard Edition of the Complete Psychological Works of Sigmund Freud.* London: Hogarth.

Jackson, T. and Beail, N. (2013) The practice of individual psychodynamic psychotherapy with people who have intellectual disabilities. *Psychoanalytic Psychotherapy* 27: 108–123.

Klein, M. (1932) *The Psychoanalysis of Children*. London: Hogarth Press.

Malan, D.H. (2001) Individual Psychotherapy and the Science of Psychodynamics. London: Butterworth.

National Institute of Health and Clinical Excellence. (2016) Mental Health Problems in People with Learning Disabilities: Prevention, assessment, and management. (NICE guideline NG54). Retrieved from https://www.nice.org.uk/guidance/ng54

O'Driscoll, D. (2009). Psychotherapy and intellectual disability. In T. Cottiss (Ed). *Intellectual Disability, Trauma, and Psychotherapy.* London: Routledge.

Rogers, C.R. and Dyamond, R.F. (1954) *Psychotherapy and Personality Change*. Chicago: University of Chicago Press.

Tyson, R.L. and Sandler, J. (1971) Problems in the selection of patients for psychoanalysis: comments on the application of "indications," "suitability" and "analysability". *British Journal of Medical Psychology* 44: 211–229.

Shepherd, C. and Beail, N. (2017) A systematic review of the effectiveness of psychoanalysis, psychoanalytic and psychodynamic psychotherapy with adults with intellectual disability: progress and challenges. Psychoanalytic Psychotherapy 31: 94–117.

Sinason, V. (1992) *Mental Handicap and the Human Condition: New Approaches from the Tavistock.* London: Free Association Books.

Simpson, D. and Miller, L. (2004) *Unexpected Gains: Psychotherapy with people with learning disabilities*. London: Karnac.

Sublette, M.E. and Novick, J. (2004) Essential techniques for the beginning psychodynamic psychotherapist. *American Journal of Psychotherapy* 58(1): 67–75.

Symington, N. (1981) The psychotherapy of a subnormal patient. British Journal of Medical Psychology 54: 187–199.

Vlissides, N., Beail, N., Jackson, T., Williams, K. and Golding, L. (2017) Development and psychometric properties of the Psychological Therapies Outcome Scale (PTOS-ID). *Journal of Intellectual Disability Research* 61: 549–559. https://doi.org/10.1111/jir.12361

Vlissides, N., Goulding, L. and Beail, N. (2016) *A systematic review of the outcome measures used in psychological therapies with adults with ID* in Beail, N. (Ed) (2016) *Psychological Therapies and People Who Have Intellectual Disabilities*. Leicester: British Psychological Society.

Chapter 11:
From Secure Accommodation to an Ordinary Life

The first thing that strikes me about the title of this chapter is the need to give a definition of 'secure accommodation' and 'ordinary life'. Both have a huge range.

Bearing in mind that one of the criteria for trauma-informed care is a safe place to live, it might follow that secure accommodation is just that – and, of course, it can be. But it can also feel like a restricted environment and, as it is often time-limited, never really feel like home.

Secure accommodation can be anything from a locked residential care home to a high secure hospital for violent offenders. I have worked at all levels.

High secure units

In the high secure facility, the feel is of a prison with doctors and nurses. All policies are there to ensure the safety of patients and staff. Everything is locked; everything is documented. There is little or no privacy.

My own experience was of very damaged, distressed and traumatised people. I never met a perpetrator who had not been a victim first. And yet most victims do not become perpetrators. Histories were painful to read and talk about. Several therapeutic interventions were offered and I was involved in the setting-up and running of a psychotherapy group, as well as offering individual therapy to some of the most distressed individuals. This therapy was all with people with learning disabilities and it was new to the establishment. The impact was noticeable and measurable. Psychodynamic approaches had previously been unavailable in the establishment but the appointment of a psychoanalyst, as well as myself, enabled some new ideas to take root.

The experience taught me that there is no one who cannot benefit from addressing traumatic early life events. It is strange to work therapeutically with deep emotional pain in an environment of locked doors, constant supervision, and lots of rules – although it is possible and needs to be developed further. Addressing early life events is not easy but most definitely is necessary and worthwhile. Sadly, some people who gravitate to high secure accommodation never leave.

Medium secure units

Medium secure accommodation is more common and there are a number of NHS and private establishments in the UK that offer this level of security. Again, lots of locked doors and restrictions on activities. Most have a time limit of two years. For an emotional developmental model of therapy, two years is the worst timeframe there could be. If people have felt safe and engaged in a therapeutic process to address their distress and trauma, at two years they will just be beginning to trust and to grow their identity. Being moved on after two years proves that no one can be trusted for the long term and people often revert back to the distressed state they were in at the time of initial detention.

Some medium secure provisions still have very strict rules and these can be experienced as harsh and even bullying. It is possible to provide emotional support in secure settings and this is what needs to happen. There are approaches that focus on building trust and working together; careful use of restraint and seclusion is needed. One thing I have always advocated is that communication must continue during restraint and seclusion. If shutting someone in a seclusion room means that the staff get a break, this provides a perverse incentive to use the seclusion room. If the staff stay at the door and maintain communication, everyone has a chance to feel heard, but in a safe way.

Another thing I have noticed in the medium secure units I worked in is that the patients know the system better than the staff. They have usually been there longer and had plenty of time to study the environment and the timetables. Staff turnover tends to be high in such units and, additionally, they will have been warned not to get too attached to the people they are looking after. It is quite common for staff to be told not to get too attached, as was the rule in the old institutions, but it works against anything therapeutic. A lot of staff members find it difficult to go against their natural urge to help and to care, whereas others get quite envious of the level of care the patients get while they themselves feel neglected and abused.

The dynamics of this sort of care environment are complex. Obholtser and Roberts in *The Unconscious at Work* (2019) would have a lot to say! Systems theory is useful in closed environments and it is always worth considering the impact of trauma on the individuals, the staff, management and the wider public. The attempt to put a lid on the pain and distress and make it criminal and punishable backfires. It is always very difficult to identify the factors that maintain a sick system. But there are some units that work well and address issues, so it must be possible. Having a shared and clear view of trauma – early trauma, in particular – can only help everyone (patients, staff, and in the wider world).

Low secure accommodation

Low secure units still have locked doors but individuals can usually go out. Sometimes, if they have progressed to being able to be trusted – and trust themselves – to come back, they can go out alone Low secure units also often suffer from the two-year rule, so the trust is broken at just the wrong time.

Some assessment and treatment units are the equivalent of low secure accommodation, as they have patients detained under the Mental Health Act, as well as locked doors. Restraint is allowed and used. There are less likely to be seclusion rooms. There may be very bare bedrooms to avoid ligature points and other potential hazards for self-harm or harm to others.

To me, secure units are more like the old hospitals, in that they are staffed by doctors and nurses with lots of paperwork and lots of rules and regulations. It is easy to see how the aim can end up being just to run a tidy unit, when it should and could be to help all the service users to address their trauma and find a way to live with what cannot be changed. If all the service users were assessed using the FAIT, it would be possible to set up care plans and groups to facilitate their emotional development into a sense of self that could be secure enough to take them back into the community.

Residential care

Residential care varies enormously. A number of providers who would prefer to offer supported living are pushed into residential care by the Care Quality Commission regulations. The registration and funding rules do not make supported living easy. Residential care facilities for people with learning disabilities are usually developed for 10 to 20 people in order to be economically viable, which then means that new people can be added any time people leave (for whatever reason).

There is no real possibility of developing the strong 'family' feel that is needed to provide an emotionally nurturing environment. It is not impossible, if individual care teams are set up and maintained, but it is hard work. Staff turnover becomes a real issue in all services. Inevitably, the secure base that John Bowlby talks about – and advocates for – becomes the place rather than the people, which was the case in the old-style institutions. There is a need for careful consideration of emotional needs in all future plans.

Supported living

Let's turn now to how a person can move from secure accommodation to supported living. This following is based on true stories – albeit several have been amalgamated so that no one can be identified.

First, I want to consider a young woman who was taken into care at a very young age after being injured by her parents. She had a moderate-to-severe learning disability and exhibited very distressed behaviour, hurting herself and others, as well as destroying property. It was not uncommon for her to be restrained by five people at the same time. Being overcome in this way was further traumatising for her.

Another young woman was traumatised by her parents' failure to provide a secure base. She had a learning disability and as a teenager was 'rented out' by her parents. She would become very distressed, needing three people to hold her in restraint. On one occasion, I was able to speak with her while she was restrained and she shouted out all sorts of things about what had happened to her. This was the beginning of her being able to move out of secure accommodation. She began to face her own needs and people began to listen to her. The abuse had been going on for her whole life.

Looking at both of them, we can see abandonment after injury on one hand, and exploitation with abuse on the other. It is difficult to accept what has happened to people who cannot defend themselves. When assessed with the FAIT, both were found to be functioning emotionally at a very early age – mainly the practising stage, with some differentiation and occasional early rapprochement behaviours. This meant that any intervention was going to require a named significant other to be available at all times, including knowing who will be there when they wake up in the morning. Putting this in place in the relevant secure units was possible but went against the usual practice. Consequently, plans to move them to supported living in the community began.

The first lady did not speak, so it was not easy to identify what she would like. A bungalow was found with a staff team trained to provide the right level of emotional support. This was comparable to the care of a one-year-old emotionally, but to the care needed for a grown person physically. It takes a bit of practice to provide the right approach, but it works. She had been used to lots of restraint and seclusion. Consideration was given to the positive benefits of being able to get away from distress and people. A safe room was put together with fully padded walls and floor, music piped in and out of range, cushions to be comfortable, and a three-quarter door to provide safety without seclusion. If she went into the safe room when distressed, the staff stayed at the door and maintained contact. As soon as she felt better, she came out and had a drink and often a cry as well. Over time, the trust grew between the support staff and the individual, with recognition and acceptance of the depth of the pain from the past. Real relationships provided the necessary emotional environment.

At the beginning of the intervention, the level of emotional development was practising and differentiation. Differentiation behaviours began to decrease and some early rapprochement behaviours were seen. She became able to see people as benign, not aggressive. The absence of restraint made a huge difference. We can only imagine what it is like to be overpowered by others. It can never be seen as therapeutic – although I do accept that sometimes it is unavoidable.

Training and support for staff

One of the biggest issues that comes to my attention from stories like this is the pressure on staff. They are on the frontline, dealing with responses to deep trauma. Inevitably, they will find their own trauma responses activated by projection. It is only with an understanding of psychodynamic approaches that the power of projection can be understood and tolerated. This is why the third element of trauma-informed care is training and support for staff.

All workers with trauma need to have, at least, an opportunity to complete training in 'All Behaviour Has Meaning'. This training looks at behavioural, cognitive, psychodynamic and systems approaches. After having the four approaches described, staff work in groups to consider which approach will be best for the person they are looking after. Ideally, this is done in groups, as it enriches the discussion.

- Very traumatised people do not respond to behavioural approaches, primarily because the main element is praise for doing things right. People with early trauma cannot value the opinion of someone else, so do not respond to praise (except maybe to be suspicious of it).
- Cognitive approaches are at the core of cognitive-behavioural therapy and depend, for efficacy, on individuals being able to 'think about' something. This requires a core self who can think about themselves and then compare those thoughts with thoughts about others and events. Very traumatised people cannot do this, especially if they are pre-rapprochement developmentally.
- Psychodynamic approaches capture the core need for attachment, emotional security, safety, and no demands. Being able to provide this takes practice but, once staff understand the basics, they can usually provide the secure base that Bowlby talks about.
- Systems approaches are always worth looking at. The bigger the organisation, the more complex the system. So, a 20-bed unit is more complex than a single person service, with the expected consequences. If a system can be drawn out in all its complexity, it becomes obvious why there are communication breakdowns, with the emotional stress that follows. David Kinsella wrote eloquently about this in the 1980s; he found that an organisation could function positively with up to 100 people but, beyond that, communication broke down. This supports the model of attachment pods for service delivery.

Working in reverse, if we can provide a stable system, the right level of emotional support, problem-solving cognitive exercises, and positive regard for appropriate behaviour, we can see what the aims are. We must always start with the right foundations; otherwise, it just goes round in circles and we are left with a pattern of progress and breakdown.

Once staff have the basic understanding, they still need a forum in which to address the complexity of the feelings projected by traumatised people, as well as their own stuff that will inevitably have been activated. Many of the people who choose this line of work have had life experiences that have led them to the field. Many of them have relatives with disabilities, which can be helpful, but they need space to explore their feelings if they are to always put their client first.

A support group meeting on a regular basis needs to be in place if possible – ideally once a week, but once a fortnight is acceptable. I always start the group by asking each member of the group to speak about something that has made them do a double-take since the last time we met. People become more observant as a group progresses and start to notice truly meaningful things that deepen their understanding of trauma and distress, as well as positive things. Everyone grows from the process, thinking develops, and the people who receive care benefit from the growing confidence of their carers.

Meeting needs going forward

It is possible to put this sort of group support into any type of provision, from all levels of secure accommodation to supported living. However, it does not seem to be readily available. This may be a reflection on the professional training that people receive and the policies put forward from the centre and authorised by NICE. It is important that there is central guidance and that policies are supported by research; however, the research that is needed to support what I am saying here is very difficult to carry out. It is not possible, ethically, to designate a control group and refuse them the care that they need. We can, however, look at the histories of people who are benefiting and we can find 'practice-based evidence' that shows the impact of care approaches based on accepting the impact of trauma and working systematically to facilitate emotional development.

Institutional care can mean treating people as less than human and this can never be right. I am concerned that the institutions will be reinvented in response to the level of need that is now becoming apparent. There seems to be a pattern developing in the 2020s of lack of response to the early identification of those in need. The waiting list for children to be assessed for Special Educational Needs and Disabilities (SEND) is huge. As is the case for CAMHS. It is not clear whether this reflects an increased incidence, a failure of early help services, a general lack of resources, or a combination of all these.

There can be no doubt that the failure to address the early trauma issues will lead to an increase in the numbers referred for secure care. Designing and advocating for trauma-informed support for children, and trauma-informed supported living for adults needs to be on the agenda for all commissioners and policy-makers.

References

Kinsella, P. (1985) *Supported Living: A New Paradigm*. London: National Development Team.

Obholzer, A. and Roberts, V.Z. (2019) *The Unconscious at Work*. London: Routledge.

Professional applications beyond intellectual disability

Chapter 12:

Disability Psychotherapy and Black Youth Knife Crime

A New Framework for Understanding and Intervention

Dr Erica McInnis

Note on terminology

In this chapter the term 'Black' is used to refer to people of African ancestry. This includes people of high skin pigmentation who may have multiple racial heritage. It is acknowledged the term 'African' is preferred by some to Black. The author is Black British of Jamaican parentage and speaks about her community sensitive to its gifts and challenges.

The urgent need to apply a new model

Knife crime involving young Black people in the UK is often framed by the media within general narratives applied to knife crime of criminality, youth street violence, and gang involvement (Vinnakota, 2022). This perspective fails to acknowledge the deeper, systemic, psychological and developmental factors contributing to many of these tragedies (Gliga, 2009; Harding, 2020; Williams, 2024). Knife crime does not require a network to gain access to weapons. Weapons of choice can be readily available in one's own home, on the internet, and in local shops. Young people (under 18 years of age), families, and schools can spend years pleading for mental health support and other support when early warning signs of perpetrators of severe knife crime emerge (Rapp, 2025; UK Home Office, 2025). They are often dismissed, ignored, or failed by services (Doyle *et al*, 2024; Memon *et al*, 2016; Sashidharan, 2003). Study of the impact of trauma, intellectual disability, and delayed emotional development upon knife crime seems lacking.

Has a reaction to the over-diagnosis of people of African ancestry as intellectually disabled (Richardson, 2005) led to under-diagnosis, no diagnosis, and no input? This has left some families bullied, assaulted, and living in fear of young people who present with extreme emotional and behavioural problems, which they experience as violence. Over-representation of Black victims of knife crime is a longstanding significant issue for some UK Black communities (London Assembly, 2020; Macpherson, 1999; YouGov, 2021). Is it when this issue affects White people, such as in the tragic killing of three White girls by Axel Rudakubana in 2024, that curtailing knife crime gains momentum (Delgado and Stefancic, 2017; UK Home Office, 2025)?

Disability psychotherapy, traditionally used to support individuals with diagnosed intellectual and developmental disabilities, has never been systematically applied to this crisis. Yet, its principles offer a powerful lens for understanding the emotional needs of Black children and young people at risk of violence. Combining the lens of disability psychotherapy with the approach of African psychology (considering the lived experiences of people of African ancestry from their perspective) is novel and the next logical step for disability psychotherapy. African psychology has a history of addressing issues important to their community, hence a focus on knife crime – given that one incident is one too many. This is important, as by reframing youth violence as a manifestation of emotional and developmental disabilities shaped by trauma, systemic racism, and social neglect, we can build interventions that prevent further harm. Applying psychodynamic theories to occurrences of violence in Black communities is not new (Wilson, 1990), whereas integrating the Frankish model to theories of early development is.

This chapter explores how the Frankish model of disability psychotherapy (Frankish, 2019) can be applied to perpetration of violence by young Black people and the role of trauma. The Frankish model of emotional development identifies five key stages of emotional development and suggests disruptions in meeting developmental tasks in these stages contribute to a lack of healthy psychological growth and resulting functioning.

Although this chapter uses the lens of disability psychotherapy to focus on emotional and behavioural problems in young Black people, it is crucial to emphasise that this does not mean that well-behaved, law-abiding, and educationally achieving Black young people do not exist and persist (House of Commons Library, 2023). Furthermore, the Black British population is highly heterogeneous, encompassing people from various countries – many of whom have high levels of achievement in education, business, and professional fields (Demie, 2021; McInnis, 2018).

A critical question: is intergenerational trauma impacting black young people?

Trauma is defined as “an emotional response to a distressing or life-threatening event that overwhelms an individual’s ability to cope, resulting in lasting psychological effects” (British Psychological Society, 2020). According to Alleyne (2022), the race-based chattel trans-Atlantic slave trade and its legacies are traumas that create gifts alongside emotional burdens for future generations. By implication, Black children experience generational trauma due to their ancestors’ experiences.

What enslavement left intact, colonisation further fractured, as colonisation also has a trauma legacy (Mullan, 2023). Following a country’s independence from colonial control, there is further trauma as nations rebuild themselves. Some have more loyalty to their former colonisers than to each other, causing further conflict and trauma – a form of splitting, internally and externally. A programme of healing from the trauma of captivity, colonisation, or what it took to liberate is still called for (DeGruy, 2005).

It would be reasonable to expect creating an emotional safe base to be of even more importance to Black children, given intergenerational trauma (Alleyne 2022). This is not to say other racial groups have not experienced intergenerational trauma, but the prolonged extent of trauma in communities of African ancestry (eg, more than 400 years of intergenerational enslavement) is perhaps of unparalleled relevance in this context.

Government pressure in the form of a hostile environment for immigrants in the UK can be a trauma for some families in terms of exposure, disclosure, lack of belonging, and impaired access to finances (Gentleman, 2019; Jeffery *et al*, 2024). Furthermore, the COVID-19 pandemic affected the mental health of young people in general, including interrupted schooling, socialisation, friendship and play opportunities, and support (Mental Health Foundation, 2021). So, it is reasoned that history, migration patterns, and systemic barriers can shape the mental health and trauma profiles of Black youth in the UK.

The impact of trauma on Black children

A sometimes-overlooked aspect of youth violence is exposure to and the impact of psychological trauma. It is likely that some young Black children who are perpetrators of violent behaviour are not emotionally functioning at their chronological age and therefore react to feelings such as rejection, disappointment, frustration, and fear, similar to a child of a much younger chronological age. Consistent management of such emotions becomes a task beyond their level of emotional ability. In short, they lack the ability to manage their anxiety independently. However, they can find access to harmful weapons to use such as knives. Potential traumas include the following:

- Systematic racism (system of White supremacy): According to Alleyne (2022), entire families experience racialised trauma that would affect access to housing, healthcare, education and employment opportunities. The impact would be felt in activities of daily living such as driving, working, gaining education, and shopping. Overwhelmed parents may not manage their own anxiety. If the family is affected, so are the children. Exclusion from mainstream education is a genuine fear. Overt racial abuse also happens, such as the 2024 riots targeted at Global Majority People. White children were arrested for racist attacks on Global Majority People, who presumably sat next to Black children the day before (*The Guardian*, 2024). What would those Black children experience in the classroom?

- Anecdotally, trauma can stem from living and thriving in areas that lack physical safety (even when there is emotional safety). Furthermore, children can experience unintentional neglect of their emotional needs when parents have multiple jobs to survive in two climates. This may be to exist in the UK while understandably sending money "back home" to support extended family in their country of origin. This can be to pay school fees to give another generation opportunities.
- As in other racial groups, some families address life situations using covert and/or overt aggression, rather than form constructive dialogue and problem-solving that can be modelled. Thus, Black children can experience trauma from witnessing domestic violence (Yoo, 2014).
- Insecure attachments: This can happen when families are spread across the world, children are looked after by the local authority to promote their safety, parents are detained in the criminal justice system or mental health system, parents are deported, and family members have insecure attachments themselves. Trauma over multiple generations can look like culture (Menakem, 2021). Insecure attachments in adults can lead to multiple intimate partners as a form of insurance policy. This means rejection is already prepared for with another partner for avoidance of 'singlehood', as anxiety cannot be consistently managed without another person (not reaching individuation according to the Frankish model of disability). The implication can be inconsistent caregiving and differing expectations from multiple 'step-parents'. The cumulative effects of different forms of oppression may make this a more salient issue.
- Undiagnosed intellectual and emotional disabilities: As previously mentioned, families struggle in particular to access mental health and other services, so – by implication – Black young people may have mental health, developmental and neurodiversity needs overlooked. It is alleged this may be due to services not wanting to 'appear racist' by over-diagnosing young Black children or due to a lack of culturally syntonic assessment and intervention tools. These are approaches that appreciate the diversity of cultures Black families operate within. Delayed or no identification of such difficulties means Black children can experience punishment and exclusion rather than understanding of them presenting with behaviours to meet a function or unmet need. Furthermore, it can hinder access to emotional regulation interventions and problem-solving assistance. It is reasoned this delay could affect the genuine self-esteem

of young Black people if they are led to believe they are 'bad', 'not trying', or 'difficult'. This gives rise to a false self that may appear very confident, hiding an unsure 'true self'.

Understanding and applying the stages of emotional development to Black children

According to Dr Pat Frankish's model of emotional development (Frankish, 2019), individuals progress through five key stages of emotional development. When trauma, intellectual disability, or neglect interferes with this process, a person may become stuck at an earlier stage of emotional development, leaving them unable to manage stress, relationships, or conflict in a mature enough way.

Understanding these stages of emotional disability can provide a crucial framework for intervention. Although the model has a symbiotic stage where the child is entirely dependent upon its mother or primary caregiver to have all needs met (Frankish, 2019), this is rarely included in the model when applied, as such an emotional stage of development is scarcely encountered.

Stage 1: Differentiation stage (a few weeks to approximately nine months old)

- A child develops awareness of parts of their own body and plays with parts.
- Their immediate environment (eg, their cot, pram, and toys) is their world.
- These behaviours are 'self-referenced' and about meeting their own needs or getting others to.
- To help a baby successfully move through this stage, primary carers need to be available and responsive

It is suggested that territorial disputes that may lead to some knife crime are engaged in by older children who have regressed to an earlier stage of emotional development where they cannot share. Others should meet their needs and, if not done, violence used to achieve these objectives.

Some children are exposed to trauma even prior to this stage – for example, in the womb. This is reasoned as mothers may experience everyday racism, less than 'good-enough' relationships while pregnant, possible parental substance use and misuse as a way to cope with life, alongside less than ideal housing. Racial battle fatigue from meeting recurring challenges can lead to low mood and anxiety, even for privileged parents. It is hypothesised that some parents may frequently resort to emotional numbing as a coping strategy when overwhelmed, making them appear cold and disconnected to the emotional needs of their children.

So, viewed through the lens of the Frankish model, babies may lack reciprocity when they try to engage with a caregiver who is overwhelmed and under-resourced. This can lead to children who struggle with basic emotional safety and are hypervigilant. If this need is not provided elsewhere, genuinely successful progress through this stage may be an issue when later life challenges are met with this insecurity. Black communities have often provided what an individual parent cannot, so the dispersal of Black families – such as when they relocate to what may be seen as 'better' areas and countries – requires the creation of communities to meet this need.

Young people stuck in this stage may display clinginess in relationships. When the significant caregiver is overwhelmed in meeting basic needs such as shelter, coupled with a lack of sufficient understanding of how racism can manifest for the next generation, children can become extremely loyal to their peer group for protection. Children may struggle with unmet attachment needs if they perceive rejection from their parents. This perception may arise from parental absence, preoccupation with their own issues, emotional unavailability, or a lack of maturity to support the child's development. The resulting distress can manifest as aggressive behaviour, with violence sometimes used to regain a sense of emotional control or dominance.

Stage 2: Practising stage (approximately nine to 15 months old)

- The child explores their environment, practising new things repeatedly.
- It is important someone is watching to reinforce and encourage continuation.

From my clinical experience, children can become stuck at the practising stage and react strongly to interruptions to their ability to diversify later. These children may appear similar to those on the autism spectrum, with obsessions and compulsions or other ritualised behaviours. The impact of trauma is proposed as a co-existing or alternative explanation. Love promotes healthy brain development. I am aware of many Black families strong in love, when everything else may be scarce. When Black children leave the family home, enter nursery, are at child-minders or clubs, they can and do experience racism and marginalisation for reasons including race. This can appear as lacking love.

For some children with overwhelmed parents, attention is given to misdemeanours rather than appropriate behaviour. Does this lay the foundations for emotional and behavioural problems to gain interactions? If this is related to knife crime, when reciprocal love is not learned as a tool to interact with others, does fear take its place? The learning from this is that all families, and in particular Black families, who can experience additional forms of oppression, need to continue focusing on love. They also need to create environments where racism is actively challenged, where they have power and agency, and where there is space for recovery and respite from the impact of racism.

Stage 3: Early rapprochement stage (approximately 15 to 24 months old)

- The child begins to 'give and take' and negotiate. The child can and does say 'no'.
- There is two-way communication and game-playing.

Children need to win to know they can win by reason and not by asserting authority. 'Win-win' needs to be experienced by the child so they can go on to replicate this in adult situations. This is a stage where resilience can be formed, for example, to rejection or disappointment. It is possible some children may struggle to tolerate the "in-between" nature of life – that is, the uncomfortableness of things not being neatly one way or the other – and struggle to understand that life is not 'all' or 'nothing'. It is theorised that this discomfort could lead to the use of weapons such as knives to force an eventuality.

They may face a situation that happens using force, which takes away feelings of uncertainty that may be difficult to sit with. This stage of development can be about gaining control and children who feel they do not receive this may grow into adults who seek control, who may – for reasons such as racism – not have as much access to non-criminal ways of being in a position of control. Black families need to continue to let their children feel confident by allowing them to win or, when their children do not win, help them cope by providing praise and compassion for trying.

Black children who lack stable caregivers or lack good-enough experiences may struggle to work in harmony with others. In some cases, they may act out aggressively to regain a sense of control over their environment. This could explain why many young people involved in violence appear reckless or unfazed by danger. They never developed the ability to return to a caregiver for emotional grounding to help with emotional regulation. Higher numbers of Black boys rather than Black girls struggling with genuine self-esteem may reflect the increased rate at which the brains of females develop (ie, girls often mature quicker) (Fish *et al*, 2019). It is also proposed that the lengthy amount of time spent on hairstyles such as braiding, weaving and locking can lead some girls to benefit from extended periods of being nurtured and counselled, with access to wisdom from elders or those with effective life experiences. This is not to say that males do not have such practices, but they tend to be more common amongst cisgendered girls.

Stage 4: Late rapprochement stage (approximately two to three-and-a-half years old)

- The child begins to realise that they are separate from their caregiver, with manageable anxiety.
- Emotional re-fuelling is needed to help the child feel confident.
- If this does not happen, there can be separation anxiety and emotional distress.
- The child needs support to navigate these conflicting emotions and learn self-soothing.
- If caregivers are unavailable, inconsistent or frightening, the child struggles to manage emotions, leading to extreme dependency or emotional withdrawal.
- The child starts to develop a more stable sense of self but still needs external reassurance.
- The child begins testing limits, seeking autonomy while still relying on caregivers.
- The child may experience anxiety and this becomes a trigger.

Some young Black children in this stage struggle with shame and self-worth. If their early environment has been rejecting, punishing as a means to shape behaviour, or abusive, they may adopt 'hyper-masculinity' and dominance as a way to protect their fragile self-esteem.

Stage 5: Individuation stage (approximately four years old)

- The child can be away from their primary caregiver, with manageable anxiety.
- The child develops a stable sense of identity and learns to manage emotions independently as needed.
- The child can engage in healthy relationships and handle conflict constructively.
- A person who never fully reaches this stage may struggle with dependency, emotional instability, and identity confusion.

Some young Black children fail to reach individuation due to ongoing trauma, lack of positive role models, and systemic barriers to emotional growth. This leads to:

- Struggles with emotional regulation (eg, overreactions to perceived threats);
- Unstable relationships (eg, difficulty maintaining friendships or romantic relationships); and
- Escapism through drugs, violence, or crime as a way to cope with unprocessed emotions.

Case study: Akua and Jamal

In the interests of respect, a pseudonym is used to illustrate application of the Frankish model. Akua is a 15-year-old girl and Jamal a 17-year-old boy; both are of African ancestry, living in London, and dating each other. Jamal, born in Nigeria, had a traumatic upbringing marked by early exposure to violence from conflict between local Christians and Muslims over dominant customs and, furthermore, from domestic abuse against his mother by his father.

At around three years old, Jamal relocated to London with his mother. During his youth, Jamal was separated from his mother and sent to a boarding school in Nigeria while she worked long hours. He reported physical abuse, including beatings with a metal pole. He begged to be returned to England but, when he returned, he struggled to reconnect with his mother and harboured feelings of rejection towards her for sending him away.

By the age of 12, he entered the UK foster care system amid concerns of neglect. His mother could not manage his aggressive outbursts. She relied on punishment when he presented with behaviours she did not approve of, such as not washing himself and not changing his clothes, but punishment seemed to escalate his behaviours and he started to hit her back when she attempted to hit him (what she considered discipline). She believed he also became passive-aggressive – for example, forgetting to take clothes off the washing line when it rained, forgetting to defrost meat, and leaving belongings where she fell over them. At this time, she was facing the pressures of trying to gain British citizenship, which required a fee of more than £1000 (plus solicitors' fees). Her employment was cleaning through an agency, when previously she had been a schoolteacher in Nigeria.

Throughout his childhood, Jamal exhibited aggressive behaviours, such as threatening peers with knives, self-harming, and expressing violent intentions towards animals. He struggled with social communication, empathy, consideration of the feelings of others, and peers said they felt ignored in his presence because he often took more notice of the workings of things in his environment than them. He was usually alone and preferred it that way. He would often take things apart, claiming he just wanted to know how they operated. In 2019, he was diagnosed with autism spectrum condition (ASC) and given an education, health and care (EHC) plan and was given six hours of additional support at school per week, as he was struggling to keep up with his schoolwork. He still struggled but, rather than not appear 'cool' or 'trendy' to the girls in his class, he just stopped going to school.

Jamal was Akua's first boyfriend. She always found him odd and did not feel safe in his company. The only reason she dated him was because all her friends spoke of having boyfriends and she did not want to be left out. Her parents worked long hours and she felt cherished and important. This mattered a lot, as she was adjusting to the loss of her grandmother who recently returned to Ghana because her visa meant she could no longer stay in the UK. Whenever she met with Jamal, she felt safer if she had her teddy bear with her. He ended the relationship by text and she asked for the return of her belongings – in particular, the teddy bear she left in his house, as she left suddenly when his mood seemed to change the last time they were together.

Akua had said to some of the girls at her school that she was not upset the relationship ended, as – although Jamal looked very attractive – it was difficult to keep a conversation going with him and he tended to repeat the same conversations. They laughed about Jamal being 'odd but nice' and better dating himself, and Jamal overheard them mentioning his name and laughing.

The pair arranged to meet for Akua to regain her items, including the teddy bear. He could tell she wanted it and he refused to give it to her. She pulled it out of his hand and ran with it. He chased her with a large kitchen knife he had brought with him and stabbed her several times. He fled the scene but was soon caught, as he lacked the skills to conceal his actions.

Akua's attachment to the teddy bear

A transitional object such as a teddy bear is typically associated with early emotional stages (rapprochement). This suggests that Akua may have been emotionally younger than her age and using the teddy bear as a source of comfort and security.

Her demand to have the teddy back may have been a sign of emotional distress rather than simple possessiveness.

Jamal's emotional detachment and violence

Jamal's violent reaction suggests low emotional development and a lack of emotional regulation strategies.

Severe early trauma may have caused him to be stuck in the practising stage, unable to handle emotional rejection and repetitive in his conversation. His violence was not just about power but an inability to process distress in a non-destructive way.

Intervention through disability psychotherapy

If both Akua and Jamal had been assessed through a disability psychotherapy lens, interventions could have included:

- Structured individual therapy to help build a secure base in the therapeutic relationship to help rebuild stunted emotional development due to early trauma and/ or losses;
- Seeing behaviours through the lens of emotional disability so that interventions in mental health or criminal justice system settings meet their emotional development needs – this is crucial to limit young people leaving services more damaged than when they arrived;
- Attachment-based interventions to build emotional security; and
- Trauma-responsive services in schools and support for families to prevent emotional crises from escalating into violence – although these services need to understand the unique strains and traumas many Black families experience, rather than intervene purely to report to safeguarding (and then, in some, cases leave).

Applying the Frankish Assessment of the Impact of Trauma in Intellectual Disability

The FAIT (Frankish, 2019) is an assessment tool – growing in use – that estimates the stage of emotional development so interventions can be tailored to where the person is at in terms of emotional development alongside chronological age. It has applications beyond people with intellectual disabilities.

If adapted to assess Black young people involved in violence, the FAIT could:

- Identify if and where they are functioning below their chronological age and estimate their emotional development stage;
- Highlight missed learning needs and unaddressed emotional disabilities; and
- Develop therapeutic interventions tailored to their emotional development instead of punitive responses.

A mandatory FAIT screening at intake for young people in CAMHs, youth detention centres, psychiatric wards, and special schools could prevent further escalation and offer early interventions.

What disability psychotherapy can offer young Black people

- A new framework for understanding violence – viewing stabbings and aggression as signs of emotional disability, development needs and trauma, rather than restricted to criminality.
- Recognition of early emotional development delays – intervening before violence occurs by offering structured emotional development support in schools and communities.
- Tailored therapeutic interventions – using non-verbal therapies such as drama therapy, music therapy, and somatic therapy for young people who struggle with verbal expression.
- A shift from punishment to structured care – placing high-risk young Black people into trauma-responsive therapeutic programmes even if in criminal justice settings.

A call for change

Disability psychotherapy has never been applied to the issue of Black youth violence – but it should be. This model is applied in theory as a forerunner to measured application in therapeutic services, which would be the next logical step, with reporting from case studies, case series, and modifications as applicable. Understanding Black youth knife crime through disability psychotherapy and emotional disability offers a revolutionary new approach. Instead of criminalising traumatised children, we must recognise stabbings, drug use, and aggression as symptoms of emotional disability – and intervene accordingly. By recognising that many young Black boys and girls are emotionally disabled by trauma, experience delayed identification of intellectual disabilities and are impacted by racial trauma, we can shift from punitive responses to structured therapeutic care.

For every young Black person who stabs someone, there is a family who begged for help and was ignored. It is time to move beyond trauma-informed care to trauma-responsive disability psychotherapy, ensuring that young Black people get the care they need before violence becomes their only option. By shifting from punishment to structured emotional development support, we can break cycles of violence and trauma.

References

Akbar, N. (2016) *New Visions for Black Men*. Florida: Mind Productions & Associates.

Alleyne, A. (2022) *The Burden of Heritage: Hauntings of generational trauma on Black lives*. London: Karnac.

British Psychological Society. (2020) *The Psychological Impact of Trauma: Theory, research, and practice*. https://www.bps.org.uk

DeGruy, J. (2005) *Post Traumatic Slave Syndrome: America's legacy of enduring injury and healing*. Milwaukie: Uptone Press.

Delgado, R., and Stefancic, J. (2017) *Critical Race Theory: An Introduction*. New York City: New York University Press.

Demie, F. (2021) *The Educational Achievement of Black African Children in England: Barriers and School Strategies*. London: Lambeth Research and Statistics Unit.

Doyle, K. and Hannigan, B. (2024) Exploring the Experience of Racialisation and Subsequent Experiences of Psychological Therapy for Black and Multi-Ethnic Clients in Ireland. *European Journal for Qualitative Research in Psychotherapy* 14: 158–174.

Fish, A.M., Nadig, A., Seidlitz, J., Reardon, P.K., Mankiw, C., McDermott, C.L., Clasen, L.S., Blumenthal, J.D., Lalonde, F.M., Greenstein, D., Giedd, J.N. and Raznahan, A. (2019) Sex-biased trajectories of amygdalo-hippocampal morphology change over human development. *NeuroImage* 204 116–122.

Frankish, P. (2019) *Trauma-Informed Care in Intellectual Disability*. Shoreham: Pavilion Publishing.

Jeffery, A., Gascoigne, C., Dykxhoorn, J., Blangiardo, M., Geneletti, S., Baio, G. and Kirkbride, J. (2024) The effect of immigration policy reform on mental health in people from minoritised ethnic groups in England: an interrupted time series analysis of longitudinal data from the UK Household Longitudinal Study cohort. *Lancet Psychiatry* 11 (3): 183–192.

Gentleman, A. (2019) *The Windrush Betrayal: Exposing the Hostile Environment*. London: Guardian Faber Publishing.

Gliga, T. (2009) *The 'Knife Crime' phenomenon - A psychological perspective on youth knife culture*. BPS Parliamentary Office. https://doi.org/10.13140/RG.2.2.14424.80643.

Harding, S. (2020) Getting to the Point? Reframing Narratives on Knife Crime. *Youth Justice* 20 (1–2): 31–49. https://doi.org/10.1177/1473225419893781

House of Commons Library. (2023) *Educational outcomes of Black pupils and students in England*. UK Parliament. https://commonslibrary.parliament.uk/research-briefings/cbp-9023/

London Assembly. (2020) *Commission on knife crime in the Black community*. Greater London Authority. https://www.london.gov.uk/press-releases/assembly/commission-on-knife-crime-in-black-community

Macpherson, W. (1999) *The Stephen Lawrence Inquiry: Report of an inquiry by Sir William Macpherson of Cluny*. London: The Stationery Office.

McInnis, E.M. (2018) Understanding African beingness and becoming. *Therapy Today* Oct: 28–31.

Memon, A., Taylor, K., Mohebati, L.M., Sundin, J., Cooper, M., Scanlon, T. and de Visser, R. (2016) Perceived barriers to accessing mental health services among black and minority ethnic (BME) communities: a qualitative study in Southeast England. *BMJ Open* Nov 16; 6 (11): e012337. doi: 10.1136/bmjopen-2016-012337. PMID: 27852712; PMCID: PMC5128839.

Menakem, R. (2021) *My Grandmother's Hands: Racialized trauma and the pathway to mending our hearts and bodies*. London: Penguin.

Mental Health Foundation. (2021) *Impacts of lockdown on the mental health of children and young people*. https://www.mentalhealth.org.uk/explore-mental-health/publications/impacts-lockdown-mental-health-children-and-young-people

Mullan, J. (2023) *Decolonizing Therapy: Oppression, historical trauma, and politicizing your practice*. New York: W.W. Norton & Company.

Nsamenang, A.B. (2006) Human ontogenesis: An indigenous African view on development and intelligence. *International Journal of Psychology* 41 (4): 293–297. https://doi.org/10.1080/00207590544000077

Rapp, J. (2025) *UK government exploited Southport attack to justify further repressive measures.* World Socialist Web Site. https://www.wsws.org/en/articles/2025/01/28/gwlk-j28.html

Richardson, B. (2005) *Tell It Like It Is: How our schools fail Black children.* Stoke-on-Trent: Trentham Books.

Sashidharan, S. (2003) From Outside to Inside: Improving Mental Health Services for Black and Minority Ethnic Communities in England. *Mental Health Review Journal* 8 (3): 22–25.

The Guardian. (2024) *'Stop letting your mum down': Five takeaways from the UK riot courts.* https://www.theguardian.com/uk-news/article/2024/aug/16/stop-letting-your-mum-down-five-takeaways-from-the-uk-riot-courts

UK Home Office. (2025) *Prevent learning review: Axel Muganwa Rudakubana.* https://www.gov.uk/government/publications/prevent-learning-review-southport-attack/prevent-learning-review-axel-muganwa-rudakubana-accessible

UK Home Office. (2025) *Crime and Policing Bill: Knife Crime Factsheet.* https://www.gov.uk/government/publications/crime-and-policing-bill-2025-factsheets/crime-and-policing-bill-knife-crime-factsheet

Vinnakota, D., Rahman, Q., Sathian, B., Mercy Bai, A.C., Deividas, N., Pellissery, V., Abdul Kareem, S.K., Hasan, M.R., Parsa, A.D. and Kabir, R. (2022) Exploring UK Knife crime and its associated factors: A content analysis of online newspapers. *Nepal Journal of Epidemiology* 12 (4): 1242. https://doi.org/10.3126/nje.v12i4.49994

Williams, E. (2024) Policing the Crisis in the 21st Century: the making of "knife crime youths" in Britain. *Crime, Law and Social Change* 82: 799–820. https://doi.org/10.1007/s10611-023-10089-8

Wilson, W.J. (1990) *Black-on-Black Violence: The psychodynamics of Black self-annihilation in service of White domination.* Brooklyn: Afrikan World Infosystems.

Yoo, J.A. (2014) Racial variations in the link between domestic violence and children's behavioral outcomes. *Children and Youth Services Review* 44: 90–99.

YouGov. (2021) *Knife crime a much greater concern among ethnic minorities.* https://yougov.co.uk/politics/articles/37079-knife-crime-much-greater-concern-among-ethnic-mino

Chapter 13: The Dementia Story

Tilly Brock

My background

To provide a bit of history, and the motivation to develop a model of care that ran alongside Dr Pat Frankish's trauma-informed model of care, I will begin by introducing myself, as well as the relationships that led to the fruition of a dementia care model.

As a child, I lived in the same situation as my mother Dr Pat Frankish – many years were spent with my grandparents within an NHS learning disability and mental health hospital/institution. I have good memories and am sure I was protected from many aspects of care at that time. However, we grew up confident in being with people who were seen as 'different'. My career began in administration and I was 28 before I began a career in nursing. My drive at that time was to work with older adults and, since qualifying in 2001, I have worked in dementia care in various environments and roles, including acute care, community care, and care homes.

Very early on in my career, I wrote a proposal to change dementia care services in my then local area and develop a memory service for assessment and diagnosis, and continued to enjoy service development throughout my career. My ambition during my nursing training was to become an admiral nurse; back in 1998, this was new and innovative. Supporting families and the network around the person living with dementia made sense to improve quality of life for the whole family and friendship networks. I was fortunate to be employed as the 72nd admiral nurse for Dementia UK in 2006, and carried on working as a specialist dementia nurse, spending 15 years supporting carers and people living with dementia.

In 2015, I left the NHS and worked for my family's care company (Frankish Psychology and Amara Care Ltd) in a sponsored admiral nurse post within social care. I consider myself very fortunate to have been given the opportunity to develop services within social care that could improve quality of life in an innovative and fun way for families living with dementia.

The initial idea was built on my own experiences and knowledge gained from the many families I supported, as well as from hearing the many times they reported that what they need is services 'all under one roof'. Families wanted a supportive service that offered different aspects of care to support both the person with dementia and family carers in a holistic and compassionate way throughout the whole and long progression of living with dementia – giving them access to someone to talk to when they needed and having one assessment only, thereby removing the need to repeat the same information to various agencies. This encompassed all stages, from pre-diagnosis to after bereavement.

It was a challenge for a nurse from a health background to begin working in social care and the networking that was natural in healthcare appeared to be very different in social care. By way of example, revalidation was an accepted part of practice in healthcare, whereas it was difficult to find a nurse willing to go through this process with me in social care. The relationships within healthcare were very different and, unless you were a commissioned service, there was reluctance to use our services. I have one specific memory of being told by a practice manager that they would not signpost families to our free peer support session, as it was facilitated by a limited company (Amara Care) – the suggestion being that we would be coercing families to purchase our services. I found this very offensive for many reasons, namely:

- It gave the impression that families were not able to think for themselves;
- There are limited services for families living with dementia and not signposting was neglecting their needs;
- Personally, I was being judged without the person understanding or asking for clarification on the model of care; and

- Making money was never the motivation to improve service for people, and it became apparent that it is impossible to be altruistic in the care sector.

Fortunately for me, I was working in a company that had previously gone through these difficulties, and coping strategies were learnt in order to progress. Also fortunately for me, as I had moved back to an area where I started my career, relationships were formed with the local memory services and they seemed happy to make referrals for carers to the admiral nurse service.

Focus on dementia care

Peggy's Place, which was a drop-in session for families at no cost (as funding was gained from the Bromhead Hospital Trust), operated in two counties as the company decided to work across county borders, unlike in health and social care. Initially, in response to the needs of those attending, I and a colleague from Pat Frankish Psychology provided day care. In 2016, the dementia 'team' now included myself and a support worker and we were able to provide hands-on practical care. We could now offer home care, carer support, training, day trips, day care, and Peggy's Place. I had begun to form relationships in both counties with various health and social care teams either by networking or by liaising with agencies to provide support for families living with dementia. Within Amara Care, we made requests to the bank, etc, for financial support. However, there was not enough support to make the model a reality.

In time, however, we recognised as a family that it was time to move away from a limited company and become a social enterprise. Dementia care did not seem to attract funding. A social enterprise would enable a company to be self-sufficient and to improve services for families, as well as give back to the community. The Peggy's World Community Interest Company (CIC) model came into fruition, with myself and my sister as directors. It was decided that there would be two directors to enable us to make decisions quickly. The first year of Peggy's World began with fundraising to a total of £11,000. During the second year, we recruited a registered manager to enable care provision, and had allocated admin funded/gifted by Amara Care Ltd gratuitously.

And so the move away from Amara Care Ltd began. The aim was to offer a holistic model of care, providing services under one roof – including day care, home care, respite care (individuals and couples supported via our home care staff), day trips, and training – and for these services to fund the provision of free services such as specialist family carer support and peer support sessions (in Peggy's Place). Our model was primarily aimed at supporting families and people with dementia during the early stages of dementia and at providing education for future care options, recognising the needs and activities appropriate for a person living with dementia. What we wanted to achieve was a self-sufficient model, not reliant on commissioning, to meet the needs of families living with dementia in the earlier stages of its progression by providing practical support (inclusive of longer-term support via emotional support).

By the end of the second year, we were providing limited home care, day care, day trips, Peggy's Place, and an admiral nurse service based within Amara Care Ltd. Our aim was to identify a building that would enable the provision of services all under one roof, so as to crete that 'one-stop shop' that families kept asking for. The decision about where was still open to negotiation and depended on finding an appropriate building.

Dr Pat Frankish, Peggy's World's 'social angel', purchased a building in 2017. This building was a former council office building and, in the 1960s, had been a local authority children's home. It was a large house in a quiet corner, with car parking and a lift already in situ! In March 2017, we held an open day for our current clients and invited local families, resulting in an attendance of 47 people (comprising people with dementia and their carers). I can recall a feeling of jubilation that local people were interested and wanted to support us. We were able to share the model of care (see Appendix 1) and gain feedback from families about what they wanted to include in the developments. However, that was short-lived, as we received an email that day to inform us – without warning – that the admiral nurse contract was being discontinued. This can only be described as deflating, given that the whole model was based on providing free specialist carer support. However, we decided to continue with Peggy's World CIC at this time.

I cannot forget to mention that we had the loveliest builder (we cannot thank him enough and never really got the opportunity to have an 'open day' on completion of all building words), who got on board with our idea and provided all the refurbishments and alterations we wanted at a lesser cost than a commercial builder. This fitted in with the idea of the building being a 'home from home' service and non-clinical. He did work when the building was empty to enable us to continue providing day care and Peggy's Place. There were some challenging times, as my nursing skills did not necessarily prepare me for being a project manager and making changes to building structures. Building alterations were ongoing in various forms, finally completing the garden area in September 2020.

We did make changes to the way we provided specialist family carer support and stopped accepting referrals from local health and social services, as they were not funding this in any way. The General Data Protection Regulation (GDPR) also came in and we wrote to all 300-plus of our families to inform them. Only the information of those who returned a signed consent to keep information was shared further. I continued to support families who were already known and returned their details, as well as details of those using our paid-for services and those who attended Peggy's Place peer support group.

Challenges to the model of care

We did have a few support visits funded by Adult Social Care for training and carer education. I am most gratified that a few carers also felt that Adult Social Care should pay for the specialist family carer support and, as a CIC, this was appreciated and helped us to continue providing 'free' services. We were also grateful that the local School for Social Entrepreneurs supported a bid for a Tovertafel table, as this was the first time financial support had been offered to us – albeit to provide an asset. As sisters and directors, we were unable to make National Lottery funding bids, which was to our detriment. The banks continued to not support developments. During the first year of our home care service, the Care Quality Comission inspection went well. The inspector was very positive about our services and the model of care, and we had a 'good' standard in all aspects of key lines of enquiry.

This is where we came into much difficulty with the Care Quality Commission, entailing an 18-month discussion about registration. The building has a large downstairs and we converted the upstairs into three en-suite double bedrooms and one en-suite single bedroom plus an additional kitchen area. Downstairs was converted into a large day area for

'Keeping Busy at Peggy's' day care service, a craft room, an office, and a wet room. However, our 'home from home' supported bed-and-breakfast model of respite care for people with dementia (and their carer, if required) became impossible unless we registered as a residential care facility. Day care was an unregistered activity but, if people stayed overnight in a bed, then we would need to register. It seemed you cannot have a home care agency and overnight stays under the same roof.

Everything about this challenged our model of care, as well as the 'home from home' feel with familiar carers and continuation of care. Also, as our home care service operated from the same base, we would have to register the same carers who would support overnight again within the residential registration. This made no sense. It felt like we were being charged to care, and people in early-stage dementia do not want to stay in residential care! An 18-month argument thus ensued. We gave in, however, as there seemed no way around the problem. The bedrooms all now needed care alarms, and we had to make the building to residential care requirements, at more cost. The patient files needed to be doubled or tripled for using the same agency but for different activities (home care, day care, respite care). I despaired at the tick-box processes in place and could not identify how services will ever change with this outdated thinking. Our local MP was supportive and we are grateful that she did speak in the House of Commons in an attempt to raise our concerns. Eventually, in 2019, we were able to have people staying overnight.

In 2019, the registered manager and I attended the Dementia Congress, with a poster presentation (see Appendix 2). Comments we received included "it's similar to the Maggie's Centre model for cancer care"[1] and "that's what families need", which provided motivation and the confirmation that we were on the right tracks.

By 2019, we were at a point where we had reduced carers to support, which provided capacity to formulate the logistical side of the business. We continued with day trips, home care, day care, Peggy's Place, and US occupational therapist Teepa Snow's training workshops for family carers and staff. Staff were all trained in the model of 'Positive Approaches to Care' from this workshop, and had contact with myself in the event of any concerns expressed about clients. Staff also received training in the trauma-

1 Maggie's Centre offers full family support, allowing carers to stay with their loved one in respite care to avoid separation and maintaining emotional support.

informed model of care and were supported if they wished to continue at higher levels. The logistics were becoming better-formed and we had HR consultants, policies and procedures, training schedules, etc, all in place. I developed a holistic assessment for each person that would continue for whatever paid-for services they received. This included recognising the Gems® model and identifying skills, life history, and relationships.

We were so fortunate that staff came to work with us because they wanted to support people with dementia. We had a few respite stays for people with dementia by themselves, but had not extended this service as yet due to staffing overnight. We accepted a rehabilitation client to stay, which was funded by health and social care. It was working! Working slowly, but working.

In February 2020, we broke even for the first time. We knew it would take time to do this; however, as a social enterprise, we did not exist to make profit for shareholders but to improve and develop services further. We had plans to open up respite from April 2020 and a staff recruitment campaign was ongoing. The building was now registered as residential. Our 'social angel' had agreed to build an extension onto the property to enable more space and flexibility within the building, plus one more respite room, and the electrics had been moved to accommodate this. The garden was still bare and awaiting completion once the building work was finished but we had a garden plan, which was developed with the clients attending day care and/or Peggy's Place.

On 17 March 2020, we closed our day care, as – owing to the COVID-19 pandemic – it was becoming too scary to continue. And then lockdown came. We prioritised home care service (ie, personal care, diet, hydration, medication, isolation) to those most in need. We furloughed the staff we could (including myself) in April 2020, once Personal Protective Equipment (PPE), etc, was sourced. Building work stopped. Peggy's World CIC was then led by my sister and the registered manager and reduced services as much as possible, as without income we could not facilitate services. The holistic model of care and support we had aimed to provide disappeared during the pandemic; however, there were positives. We continued to recognise carers and supplied them with flowers during Carers' Week. Afternoon teas were provided to all our clients for the D-Day celebrations, as we would have normally had a party at Peggy's Place.

Following lockdown and the reopening of services, we began cautiously with day care. Our client group had reduced, sadly. The local infection control and prevention team visited and our 'home from home' environment became a clinical, plastic space. We were not able to use upstairs and downstairs at the same time, owing to the movement of people, and made the decision to continue to reopen day care in the belief that this would meet most families' needs due to people being closed up at home for some time. I returned on a part-time basis, as financially this was the most prudent decision for the business. The fun was gone. The building felt empty. As a company, we were very conflicted at times about what to offer and did not wish to be causing harm or passing on infection to vulnerable elderly adults.

As part of a team, I will be forever gratified by our staff's compassion and caring for all of the clients. The torment that staff members went through during this time never really felt recognised enough by local health and social care providers. The clients returning to day care did not appear to feel as sad about the environmental changes; they were happy to be back together.

I was very torn at times between my director's responsibilities and those of a nurse. I felt that the whole model seemed to disappear and did not feel confident that we could get it back. The model could not work without income and, given that our clients were some of the most vulnerable in our society, I did not see it changing. There had been so many deaths and losses during the pandemic. I had also battled my own health issues in 2019 and was tired, as my sister had similar issues two years earlier. As directors, we made the decision that – as I was the most expensive member of staff and able to find work away from Peggy's – I would leave and return to the NHS and left Peggy's World CIC in March 2021.

What I had hoped for was to be able to provide a model of care that understood the needs of people living with dementia and to provide ongoing support for family carers in a positive way. In line with the Frankish model and the Gems® (Teepa Snow) model, we were able to formulate an eclectic model of care to provide throughout the whole progression of dementia and, following bereavement, recognise skills gained by families and offer the ongoing involvement to enable them to educate others if they wanted.

We wanted to be able to offer support pre-diagnosis and having a mental health nurse within the services enabled recognition and enabled families to take the evidence to GPs for a referral to be made. I had not yet reached a stage where Peggy's Place could make a direct referral to the memory service. I also wanted to partake in research involving people living with dementia and to research their regression, using the child development model as in line with the Frankish model of care. As a one-stop shop, there could have been opportunities throughout the disease's progression to develop evidence-based practice as well as a model that could be implemented in other geographical areas around the country.

Peggy's World continues today under the umbrella of Amara Care Ltd and continues to provide day care, home care, and Peggy's Place (still free!). We took the decision to make Peggy's World CIC dormant in 2021. We were commissioned in 2021 to provide a local dementia advisory service by the local authority, which supported ongoing services; this was a regular income, which was needed coming out of the pandemic. It was appreciated that we were being recognised as a provider.

However, this contract was terminated and another complaint ensued. Fortunately, the local authority did continue this service provision via an alternative provider. Peggy's World CIC did not want to rely on being commissioned for contracts, as our whole model was about being self-sufficient – ie, people-led for the people that need the support – but this contract did offer some financial security for a short period. The bounce-back loan needed repaying. At this time, as directors, we made the decision to close Peggy's World CIC and to run the remaining Peggy's services via my sister's company (Amara Care), as it felt important not to withdraw services to those we did serve.

Case study: Faye and Peter

As an admiral nurse, I supported the wife of a gentleman diagnosed with demenia with Lewy bodies. I will name this couple Faye and Peter, and their daughter Alice. Initial support was around diagnosis and coping strategies. I would meet Faye at a local garden centre, as she was not able to talk openly in front of Peter. Alice lived away and there was no formal care in place at this time. Peter was able to be left alone at home for short periods of time and was safe. Faye had spoken about her previous relationship with Peter and had described him as controlling. Faye had not had money independently and he kept records of spending, outings, etc. Faye had stayed with Peter because she was not financially able to leave and because she wanted them to remain a family. Faye was now in the position of caring for someone she did not want to care for.

This support – being emotional and educational support primarily – went on for approximately two years, before Peter declined and became hostile towards Faye, both physically and verbally. Faye would arrive looking drawn and tired as we discussed care options. Peter was also under the care of the memory services; however, there was no provision of practical support. When they attended Peggy's Place together, Peter was engaging and had a sense of humour, and people saw a different person to whom he was at home. A referral was made to Adult Social Care with a view to home care services but the financial assessment took so long and, before any formal care was in place, I received a phone call from Faye's sister (whom I had not met previously), stating that Faye had broken down.

I visited Faye that day and requested emergency respite for Peter, explaining to him why Faye needed a break – and that, at present, this would be the quickest way – and he agreed. Fortunately, the memory services and social care responded. As Faye was not sleeping, I spoke to Faye's GP to request some sleep medication and collected this from the pharmacy. Faye was not able to speak clearly nor eat and drink, her face was grey, and she made no eye contact, did not change her clothes or take care of her own personal care needs, and was what can best be described as "like a zombie". She was not using alcohol, however, and I visited Faye daily for five days. Meanwhile, Peter had gone into respite and had settled reasonably well. Faye's sister had been closely monitoring and supporting her with medication, etc. Faye's sleeping improved and, even though she had no recall of the beginning of the week, she was now able to talk and listen.

Accessing mental health support for Faye would take time and Dr Frankish had agreed (on a pro bono basis) to support Faye, owing to my concerns for her mental health. Faye was seen three times, and improved week by week. After six weeks, Faye had regained control of herself and I reduced my visits to twice weekly, and so on. Faye was still fearful of visiting Peter and we talked about how this might be possible with her sister's support. The decision was made for Peter to remain in care full-time. Faye did manage to gain confidence in visiting Peter and maintain the relationship she felt she needed to with him, while her and her daughter found a status quo that they could all continue to live with.

Peggy's model enabled support at the right time, in the right place, for the right people. There were no costs to Faye and her family and Peggy's had no financial gain. Faye is able to continue her life. She has no recall of the events of that week and is appreciative of the support. She is aware that, without Peggy's, it could have been a different scenario and – as she herself puts it – she may not be alive.

Case study: Vera and Simon

The example that follows concerns Vera and her husband Simon, who has dementia and is one of Peggy's longest-running clients. Vera continues to volunteer to facilitate Peggy's Place to this day, which is now facilitated under the care of Amara Care Ltd.

A new referral came into Amara Care in 2015 for a carer to take a gentleman out walking, as he had dementia. Simon was self-funding and they were a younger couple who had not reached state-pension age. I visited with the current home care manager from Amara and we recognised that Vera currently had her own physical health issues. As he was self-funding, she felt unsupported in navigating the care system. Simon was diagnosed with young-onset Alzheimer-type dementia and had particular difficulty with perception and co-ordination. We explored care options and shared the local support systems in place. We agreed to take Simon out for a weekly walk with a local Health Walk initiative. In the capacity of paid carer, I continued to support this activity, maintaining regular contact and staying longer with his wife when we returned home. Our support worker continued when she commenced work for us. Vera and her husband attended Peggy's Place and suggested supported day trips, which we then facilitated.

Vera did not have the confidence to go out with him by herself without support and no family were available to provide this. Vera was happy to pay the costs incurred to improve quality of life for them both. Simon declined as expected and we continued supported walks for as long as possible. The group we went with became familiar and concerned when inevitably we had to discontinue owing to his decline. In 2019, he was still able to come on our day trips and we reduced the time out to enable Vera and her husband to attend as his needs changed.

Vera and Simon continued to attend Peggy's Place once a week until, in 2020, he became unwell. Sadly, he was admitted to hospital at the beginning of lockdown and moved to a care home, where he died. Our staff group attended his funeral and continued to offer support to Vera and include her in any Peggy's World activities.

When our services reopened, Vera was invited back as a volunteer, which she was thankful for. Today, she continues to volunteer at Peggy's Place and support the families it supports. Everyone has happy memories of Vera and Simon – in particular, the Bertie (mini-) bus day trip, when we broke down and ended up in a champagne bar. There was so much laughter and fun and the improved quality of life was immeasurable.

On the horizon

In summary, the eclectic model of care that Peggy's World CIC developed enabled free specialist family support and provided holistic care for both the person with dementia and their family carers and friends. Unfortunately, it never came to true fruition, owing to various obstacles. We will never know if, in time, the initial aims of the CIC would have been recognised as a workable model that was cost-effective and could be duplicated in other areas. It does feel as though Peggy's has come full circle since it started in 2015, continuing to offer much-needed support to families' lives via day care, home care and Peggy's Place. The staff still have the same compassion for and understanding of how a person living with dementia progresses.

On reflection, I will use the boat analogy. I joined a ship, the good ship Amara Care Ltd. However, the ship became too full of passengers, and I left on a little boat that floated alongside Amara Care Ltd and Pat Frankish Psychology until such time that I could afford a bigger boat/small ship called Peggy's World CIC. Peggy's gained more passengers and supporters who travelled with us. However, there were icebergs that needed to be navigated, such as the Care Quality Commission, local health and social care services, business support, building costs, and – to some extent, due to the directorship – family issues.

Within a few years, we found our way through rough seas and it was looking clear ahead until the biggest iceberg came into view – known as COVID-19 – and we halted and limped along for a while as best we could on the good ship Peggy. Fortunately for Peggy, the good ship Amara was still alongside us (just out of sight) and rescued the passengers still on board Peggy. These days, Peggy stays in the sea, quietly resting. Maybe the time will come to start the engine again. But this will only happen when dementia care is recognised as needing substantial investment to reduce the highest cause of death in the UK and when care staff are valued for the contribution and innovation they bring to the care and services arena.

Resources for this chapter are available to access online:
www.pavpub.com/therapeutic-care-for-people-with-intellectual-disabilities-and-emotional-needs-resources

Personal perspectives

Chapter 14:
The Staff Story – Personal Perspectives

The staff have been key to Amara Care's successful delivery of trauma-informed care. It is important to know how they feel about being involved in the holistic model of support. Kelly Hunt, one of Amara Care's administrative support staff, spoke to some members of staff and asked a few key questions. What follows is a summary of their responses.

How long have you been with the company?

Some of the staff working within Amara Care have been with the company since it first started in 2004. Janice has been with Amara Care since Pat Frankish and Amanda Brock bought the first property. Chris has also worked for Amara Care from the beginning – although he did take a year out.

Terrie has been with Amara Care for 19 years and Cathy has worked for the company for 15 years, whereas Christine, Mel and Kelly have all been with the company for 17 years. Carol and Tracey have been with Amara Care for nearly 12 years and six years, respectively, but Tracey did agency work with the company for two years prior to that.

Elaine is a past employee who worked for Amara Care for roughly 14 years before her retirement.

Have you done similar work before?

The staff team have a mixture of experiences. Some have previously worked within caring or support work with individuals with learning disabilities; others have been completely new to this line of work but may have had some experience with someone within their life whom they have supported. Many had strong links with people with learning disabilities and have since thrived within the company.

Mel left school and chose caring as her career and has been caring ever since. Tracey had 10 years of experience in care before Amara Care, Terrie had three years working in a residential care home prior to joining Amara Care, and Christine also had experience working within residential care and in care homes before working for Amara Care. Chris worked at Rowan House before Pat and Amanda bought it and converted it into the home it is now.

By contrast, Kelly was completely new to support work – although she had supported her family with their different needs. She was given all the relevant training and support and is now a service manager within the company.

Similarly, Elaine had never worked in care; her previous careers were working at a local factory and running pubs. She had relatives who had Down syndrome, so she felt that this was the career path for her. She always felt a connection to people with additional needs; if she was in a café, she would smile at them, and this mostly ended up in a conversation. Elaine wished she had gone into support working earlier in life because it brought her so much joy.

Prior to Amara Care, Janice worked in many places (including an office, a shop and a factory) and was a cleaner at one point. A colleague once mentioned becoming a carer to her own grandmother but, in the end, Janice offered her help – to which her colleague agreed – and this is how she started her support work career. She later contacted Amanda and has been at Amara Care ever since.

Carol was also new to care when she joined the company, having been an IT tutor before becoming a support worker. Cathy had previously worked with children, providing after-school activities. Some of these children had learning disabilities and she used sports to encourage engagement.

Can you talk about what is good or different (or both) in what Amara Care provides?

In relation to her previous experiences within the caring role, Mel believes the company is absolutely brilliant and that is why she has been with Amara Care so long. The clients are well looked after and their needs are met, as staff are given all the training to help with the clients' needs. Mel states: "Overall, Amara Care is just the best company I've ever worked for."

Kelly believes the company to be unique in the way it supports the clients, giving them the opportunity to access therapy alongside their day-to-day support. She says: "I've never worked for a company that supports the client as a person and does not just focus on their learning disability."

Tracey is similarly amazed at how the support meets the clients' individual needs, as well as by the access to psychological support. Terrie also values that each service is tailored to the individual and that psychological support is offered when they need it but is available to staff as well.

Elaine spent many years with the company and had several different roles; she talked about how different the work was at the beginning. She stated that initially it was like a care home but, as the company transitioned towards an independent living ethos, those were the best years of her life. The staff began teaching the clients how to do things for themselves (eg, making a cup of tea), then helped them progress to more complicated life skills, such as cooking. Elaine explained how she used to support the clients to ensure that they used the correct chopping boards while cooking. "They were the happy days – the clients were valued, we valued them, and they valued us," she reminisced.

Christine believes that the clients are well cared-for and that Amara Care takes on clients with more complex needs that other companies would not attempt to support. "I think the care and support we give is great and the company is good to work for," she says.

Cathy also reflects upon the support provided by Amara Care and how the company takes on the challenge of supporting clients refused by others. "Amara Care provides a safe and caring environment that allows clients time to heal and develop a sense of self," she says. "We offer continuity of care, allowing for relationships to develop."

A lot of the work Amara Care does ensures that the company promotes independent living for people, which Chris singled out as a highlight of the support provided. Janice emphasises that Amara Care recognises the client's needs and capabilities and support them to achieve the best they can and to live a meaningful life. Carol also identified that staff are unique in their approach, using Amara Care's bespoke model to enable an individual to live an independent and meaningful life. The training provided is relevant to all staff and additional training is sought out when it is needed to support Amara Care's clients.

Can you describe the model of support and does it work?

Amara Care uses the singular Frankish model, which is the foundation of and encompasses the ethos of the company. When asking staff what they believed the model to be and whether it works, a mixture of responses was received.

Firstly, the model highlights four main components – namely, the secure base, the staff team (the "significant other"), staff training, and psychological or therapeutic support. When asked about the model, Carol was able to clearly identify each essential point. She stated that a secure base comes from providing:

- a home to live in as long as the client needs it;
- the availability of a staff team that understands the role of the significant other (who will be there on a regular basis), meets the needs of the clients and provides that nurturing environment;
- such people to be trained and supported themselves; and
- finally, psychological support to help people who have trauma in their lives (some clients may need this more than others).

Cathy clarified: "The model includes providing a significant other in the form of a staff member that will provide continuity of support and allow for relationships and emotional growth. In most cases, the emotional development has been halted owing to early trauma." She mentioned that the Frankish model is simple in that a safe and secure base must be provided for progression to happen; however, this can take a long time for some individuals.

Mel highlighted that the Frankish model is used daily, it works, and a difference can be seen in the clients that shows how they have progressed over the years. Kelly also believes that the model works and its focus on providing psychological support is essential for supporting Amara Care's clients.

Tracey relayed that the Frankish model works for each individual and focuses on their emotional development and needs. Terrie believes that the model "gives a person-centred approach rather than a one-size-fits-all approach", thereby "helping to cater to everyone's needs". Christine also agrees that the model works and highlighted that the client that she supports is a living example of the model working.

Elaine was proud of the Frankish model when she worked for Amara Care: "We weren't like other places locally; we provided the best. We cared more about what we were doing and the things the client could achieve. We never labelled our clients as bad, we wanted to understand why they had certain behaviours and, once we knew that, it made it clear why they behaved in certain ways and we could help them."

When Elaine worked for Amara Care, the psychologist was able to use appropriate terminology and made things clear for all to understand and follow. "We also had a lot of input from Amanda," she says. "We were able to go out into the community more and more with the clients and they began to build friendships outside the company or they became part of the community."

Similarly, Janice found that the focus on psychological support, the belief that all behaviours have meaning, and assessing the client to find their stage of emotional development – as well as working with their capabilities – enable them to live their best life. She believes that this approach works the best, whereas Chris believes the model to work for some individuals more than others.

Anything else you would like to add?

Mel wanted to add that she is happy in her job and that, if there are any issues, management is very supportive. Kelly wanted to mention that the company is so different in all areas but that "no matter where you work within the company you have support".

Elaine is so proud of all the clients she supported over the years and so amazed by how much they learned. She was honoured to support one client during their palliative care and was given lots of support from management. Elaine stated that she will never forget any of the clients she has supported and that she misses them all.

Conclusion

Overall, Amara Care will embrace the challenge of supporting the complexity of each of those individuals whom other providers would otherwise be unable to support. It is clear that Amara Care has a unique way of supporting people with learning disabilities by using the Frankish model. The staff's understanding that 'Behaviours Have Meanings' and of the importance of emotional development throughout the company ensures that the clients live meaningful lives.

The staff are trained to use the Frankish model, interventions and approaches and they take great pride in the support they provide – often staying with the company for years. Staff members appreciate and understand the importance of having that person-centred approach to support and having the input of a psychology team for the clients as well as the staff.

As a company, Amara Care offers opportunities for professional growth and will enable people with no experience of working within the care/support sector to progress into this line of work, by providing all essential training and information.

This is pioneering work, and we seek to spread the word to others. We have a training arm and provide training to other individuals and organisations. We also host a Community of Practice and are pleased to find other organisations providing support with a similar level of understanding of emotional disability caused by early trauma. Some of the contributors to this book are informed followers. There is a need to reach more people.

Chapter 15:
Sylvia's Story

Carol Hall

Sylvia was born in October 1957 and had three sisters. They all lived with their mum and dad in the town of Mossley in Tameside, Greater Manchester. Sylvia attended both primary and secondary school in this area, where she was considered to have difficulties with her language skills and was potentially being bullied by other children in the schools she attended.

Amara Care's senior staff went to visit Sylvia before she was relocated to a small town in north Lincolnshire and were happy that we could support her with her needs, that we could work with her and the psychology team, and that we could hopefully give her a meaningful life and the support that she required. It was going to be hard work but the team she had in place were all up for this challenge.

Sylvia came to Amara Care in September 2013 after spending many years in different care settings. She lived in a flat upstairs with two other female housemates, with whom she shared a kitchen and lounge, but she had her own bedroom and bathroom.

I remember my first day as a new member of staff going into Rowan House as though it was yesterday. I was presented with a lady who would not get out of bed, did not want any breakfast, told staff she would have her medication when she felt like it (ie, not when staff asked her to take it), and would swear at staff members while telling them to get out her room and to leave her alone.

I could see this was going to be a very long first day in care, but the manager at the time and I persevered with her, using softly spoken words and reassurance that everything would be okay. Eventually, after about six hours, we managed to get her to take her medication, have some breakfast, take a shower, and get dressed.

Over a period of between six and eight months, day-in and day-out, the staff team soon learned that Sylvia liked consistency in her daily life. With constant reassurance, she began to tolerate us in her bedroom and would get up in the morning when we asked her to, take a shower, have her medication, and choose her breakfast (which was always porridge at that time).

After a few months of working with Sylvia, she became less volatile towards staff and I can only describe it as a small breakthrough in her ability to understand that we were not there to fight with her but to help her develop both emotionally and physically. Slowly but surely, each day it became easier to work with Sylvia – although some days were harder than others. She always had a smile if she was in a good frame of mind; if she was not, then we had better watch our step! She could have a few choice words for us!

It took a lot of tenacity and using the training in the company's model of therapeutic approach to work with Sylvia in order to get the best from her and give her the best possible care so she could have the most meaningful life possible for her.

She would also have input from Amara Care's psychologists, who would would come along and talk to her on a regular basis. They would also work with the staff team to help us understand her emotional development and how to work with her using the Frankish model, which has four essential components, as follows:

- a secure base – having a property to enable a person to live there as long as needed and for it to be repaired if damaged;
- a staff group – members of which can meet the need for someone to always be present and have been trained in how to provide a nurturing environment;
- staff training – all staff who work with the person must be fully trained, understand the Frankish model (FAIT), and realise the importance of

the 'significant other' who will be with that individual on a regular basis, as well as be able to identify that individual's development and how to interact at the correct level to enable them to both feel and be safe; and

- psychological support – all people are different and some will have had such severe trauma in their lives that they will require individual psychotherapy to address whatever issues they may have.

With all this in mind, the staff were able to work with Sylvia in accordance with the Frankish model and ensured she was always safe and felt safe, had the correct environment to live in, had the correct trained staff team in place and had the psychological support for the more than 10 years that she was with us.

When Sylvia first came to us, staff were not allowed to touch any of her things without asking her first, as she thought we were going to steal them. She told me a story once about a new jumper she had been bought and how she saw another client, in the place she lived before, wearing it. She really disliked that and thought we would do the same. We reassured her every day she was with us that we would not do this. We always gave her a time when she would have her clothes back after they had been washed, dried and ironed.

She also would not allow anyone to touch her and would often lash out and try to scratch if she felt threatened. Over the years, she became more tolerant of this and one day she asked me for a hug. I was thinking: "Dare I? Should I? Will she try to grab me?". But I gave her that hug and never looked back. Every time I finished my shift, I would go and tell her I was going home and that I would see her tomorrow. This would always be followed by her asking "Can I have a hug before you go?" and, of course, I always obliged. The delight and the smile on her face was always for me the sign of a great step in supporting Sylvia's emotional well-being and that I had made a difference in her day.

Her washing was her prize possession and she would always want to know when she would get it back. Staff always reassured her she would get it all back when it was washed and dried. Sylvia would want to know how long it would take and we always gave her a timeframe to satisfy her need for this knowledge, as it was important to her. Although a lot of reassurance was given over the 10 years Sylvia was with us, the feelings she felt over her washing never changed. We can see this as associated with her primary trauma, which almost certainly involved someone taking her clothes.

Sylvia would always want her clothes put in the wardrobe in a particular order, her personal file on the floor next to her shoes, and her toys on her shelf so she could see them all. Her TV would always be playing the KISSTORY radio station; she loved that radio station! All her things had to be in a straight line on the floor in front of her wardrobe or she was not a happy bunny! I am sure this gave Sylvia the confidence to know her staff team would be working for her and not against her and – through this consistent approach – I do feel that Sylvia developed her own new personality, which was positive and very different from the lady I first met on that first day in care.

After a while in our care, we encouraged her to go and do her shopping on a weekly basis. Two staff would go with her in her car and she would push the trolley around the supermarket, picking up items that she liked to eat. Custard cream biscuits, Mars bars, pork pies and cheese were always the go-to for Sylvia and she was happy that she was able to pick them herself. This also gave Sylvia choices that I believe she had lacked in the past and, again, was part of her emotional development and our person-centred approach.

Sylvia always liked to have fun with her staff and this is when she and I began to bond. We would laugh and joke about a range of subjects. She would also tell the staff lots of stories about what she used to get up to in her younger years, with explicit sexual explanations of her encounters with different men. Because we never told her she was being rude or that we did not want to listen, and never judged her, she was able to share these stories. I think she really enjoyed telling these stories over and over again and the content was always the same. After quite a few months, she began to have that same bond with me and the staff team. She trusted us! She trusted that we were not going to harm her in any way but, rather, were there to support her and be one of her significant others and to keep her safe from harm.

I remember one day I picked up her brush and asked her if she would like her hair brushed and, to my surprise, she said yes. This had never happened before, as she would not tolerate anyone touching her hairbrush let alone brushing her hair. I was in shock! After I had brushed her hair, I asked her if she wanted to brush mine, expecting her to say no and swear at me. Again, I was amazed that she said: "Yes, but you're not using my hairbrush. Go get your own!" This made me giggle, so off I went to get mine and she sat there quite happily brushing my hair. This was a big step forward, in my opinion, and showed that taking a calm approach with her was working. After that, she often asked to have her hair brushed.

Sylvia also wanted to know on a daily basis who was coming on shift and who was doing the sleepover, so the team decided to make her a schedule and hang it on her wall to make sure she always knew. She would still always ask, though. This did make us laugh and I would say to her: "You tell me." Sylvia would giggle and tell us who was coming on shift next. This was part of the continuing person-centred approach to make Sylvia feel safe in her environment.

I remember talking about her moving from Rowan House to a bungalow of her own with another female client. Oh, she was over the moon to be living in her own home and always have her own staff team in the property with her. It was an exciting time for Sylvia and she was always asking "When am I going?", "Are you coming too, CH?", and "Where are we going to?".

Sylvia moved into her new home in July 2014 with another female. She had all her own possessions around her, including her beloved toys, handbags, pictures and books, and of course her TV was always playing KISSTORY radio station. She would dance sat in her chair, knew all the words to most of the songs that came on, and loved to hold staff's hands and have a dance. These were truly positive times and showed that not only did she trust her staff team but also that the model was working.

Sylvia loved nothing more than going shopping and getting an ice-cream on a nice Saturday afternoon. It was always chocolate with a flake on top. We would sit in the car and enjoy it and have a few laughs about anything that came to her mind. It was usually something that I did not expect to ever hear but it always made us giggle one way or another.

She had numerous toys and was always asking to swap one thing for another – at times, trying to persuade staff to let her have more than she had agreed to. She was as sharp as a button and knew who she could wrap around her little finger.

Her mobility was quite irregular at this time and did require staff to assist on occasion in getting her from her bedroom to the dining room table for meals. I remember once both ladies were sat at the table glaring at one another as they were eating their meal. All of a sudden, I heard "Oh, hellloooo, cauliflower" followed by "Hello, cabbage". I thought they were talking to the vegetables on their plates but, no, they were talking to each other. I heard lots of laughter after this, each and every time they sat together at the table.

Over the years that followed, Sylvia's mobility deteriorated, and she would always need staff to assist her in moving from one place to another (bathroom, bedroom, lounge, dining room). She had a habit at times of putting herself on the floor for no reason other than she enjoyed the ambulance crew coming to get her back up and onto a chair or her bed. One night she asked me to assist her back to her bedroom and just as we got to her bedroom door, we both fell on the floor. Oh, what laughter was had that night, as she said to me: "What you doing on the floor with me? The ambulance man won't get you up." We laughed so much together that evening and I assured her I could get up myself. I gave her a pillow and a blanket to keep her warm and she was grateful that she would be warm until the ambulance arrived. She never forgot this time and often reminded me of it – sometimes several times a week – and she would always think it was funny.

With the issues of mobility and not being able to get into the bath, as it was a very small bathroom, the company bought a bungalow with a wet room and moved Sylvia into this property with another female client. This property also had a ramp outside to enable easier access for Sylvia to get outside, as by this time Sylvia was in a wheelchair because her knees were always playing her up with arthritis. This also made it easier for staff to take her out on daily trips to the shops and she always had to have a cup of coffee or some lunch while she was out. She loved going to the local ice-cream parlour on a sunny day for an ice-cream and we went several weekends in the summer when I was on shift with her.

Sylvia loved her new bedroom. We decorated it in her favourite colour and put up some of her pictures of butterflies that she loved. She had new bedroom furniture and a chair that was also in her favourite colour. She became good friends with her housemate, who would always go in and say good morning to Sylvia and the response was always reciprocated.

Her housemate would get shouted at to come into Sylvia's room by Sylvia and asked to go to the garage and get her a toy. The housemate knew that Sylvia was only allowed a swap a day and would say: "You know I can't do that." Sylvia would chuckle to herself and then shout at staff. What a sense of humour she grew to have... We all loved it!

Another fond memory I have was of her 60th birthday, when we threw a birthday party for her and invited all her friends and family. Not only did she agree to come into the dining room (she usually never wanted to leave her bedroom), she would ask staff: "Have you bought me a present?" To have some fun with her that day, I said: "No, I haven't, Sylvia." She gave me the most disgusted look and asked me to leave but I could not tease Sylvia anymore and told her: "Of course I have." I kindly handed over the gift and Sylvia told me: "I knew you wouldn't forget." Then she smiled at me and, oh, how my heart melted that day.

Sylvia had a wonderful family who were always supportive of the staff and would answer any questions we had about Sylvia. They always came to visit her monthly and Sylvia loved the visits, as she knew they were coming and would say to staff (and I quote): "What is Heather going to bring me?" Her sister Heather would travel all the way from her home in Manchester to come and visit, often with other members of the family. After Sylvia had got what Heather had brought her, she would ask her sister what time she was going home, which was usually after about half an hour. This always was a joke to Sylvia and she would often laugh when staff would say "but Heather has only just got here".

They say professional boundaries should not be crossed but Sylvia became such a part of not just my life but the life of every member of staff who had interactions with her that she was like a member of our family. We did everything we could to ensure that she led a happy and meaningful life and enjoyed every second of that life while she was with Amara Care. The consequences of trauma were always there, but she was able to grow into herself with acceptance and love.

Sylvia sadly passed away on 2 March 2022. She is still missed to this day by all her friends, family, staff team, and everyone at Amara Care.

Chapter 16:
Susan's Story

I first met Susan when she was living in a care home. She was a wheelchair user and had no control of her lower limbs. She could talk, but rarely did, and sat looking very dejected. I had been asked to see her, as staff were concerned that she was very unhappy and possibly depressed.

My first visit produced little in the way of information or encouragement. She was very withdrawn and appeared to have no hope for the future. A search of the records revealed that she had severe cerebral palsy as a result of oxygen starvation at birth. She had spent the first months of her life in an incubator in the special care baby unit. She later told me, when she felt able to talk about it, that she had been moved out of her incubator when a high-profile multiple birth had occurred. She appeared resentful of that, implying that she may have recovered more if that had not happened. I do not think that was the case but we will never know.

We began a therapeutic relationship, meeting once a week for an hour. Susan organised transport to come and see me, as she wanted privacy for her sessions. It soon became clear that she was a very angry young woman. She was not accepting of her disability, the reasons for it, the treatment she had received, or her present living arrangements. I had met very angry people before, but this was extreme and her additional sense of entitlement added to the pressure to make things right.

Clearly, nothing I could do would alter the physical disability, so the work became a process of adaptation, acceptance and taking control of what could be controlled. The trauma occurred very early, in the differentiation stage of emotional development, and was compounded by never having been understood as a traumatised person. Intellectually, she was much more able – although not able to process the trauma, which was at a pre-verbal level.

Susan was able, over time, to form a relationship and develop a level of trust that allowed for some therapeutic processing and gains. She was able to tell me about her family, as well as her feelings of being a nuisance and not wanted, and then a major trauma when her father died. He had been Susan's main support prior to his demise, providing more than either her mother or her sisters did. Susan had been left without proper physical care until social services had placed her in the care home, where she did at least have her basic needs met. People were aware that Susan was very unhappy and she was prescribed antidepressant medication. The side-effects led to drooling and a general malaise. These were reduced and stopped after she engaged in therapy.

It soon became apparent that Susan was very strong-willed and had the infantile omnipotence that corresponds with very early trauma. She could use her intellect to make sure that people knew what she wanted, when she wanted it, and how she wanted it. Support staff struggled.

There was a general expectation that Susan would be grateful for the care she received. In all the years I knew her, it was clear that she was not able to feel gratitude because at no point in her life did she ever get what she wanted, which was to not be disabled. At the emotional level of a very young baby, she could not be grateful. You need to reach the stage of having an individuated self before you can put others' feelings before your own. That was unlikely to ever be achieved, but progress towards it was considered possible.

An opportunity arose for Susan to move into a purpose-built bungalow, fully adapted for wheelchair access and with ceiling tracking for hoisting. This was a supported living option with through-the-door staff support; therefore, a move on from residential care. It was in her hometown, too, so theoretically could lead to more contact with her two sisters. However, it was unlikely that staff or sisters would fully grasp her emotional needs and this proved to be the case. Susan had been on the working party that had designed and commissioned the facility and was quite proud of her achievement some of the time.

Support staff – good, well-intentioned people – could not understand why Susan was always demanding and never happy or grateful. The turnover rate was high. Susan always wanted the staff member who was not there and all felt rejected. They did manage to maintain enough support for several years but the providing agency had to use all of their staff to share the emotional strain.

One of Susan's sisters had two children and brought them to see their auntie. As a consequence, they started to go out to the shops together. Susan was always the one who paid. She wanted to have a relationship if possible, so continued for some time to accept the exploitation. It is likely that the sister carried pain from the impact of Susan's disability on her own childhood. The complex emotional factors could not really be resolved.

I remember one occasion when Susan had a hospital appointment and asked me to go with her. I had to change a lot of arrangements to be able to do so but agreed, as I thought she may not go if I did not. We got there (Susan arriving by taxi) and waited. And waited. They had said that she must have a full bladder for the scan and, of course, that made waiting too hard. So, she left without seeing the doctor or having the scan. I must admit I struggled not to be angry that day but, on reflection, could see that it fitted into the same category as all the problems. Her experience of being kept waiting was confirmation that no one cared, with an infantile impotence that "my needs come first". Of course, there is no point in being angry. Had she been a very young baby, she would almost certainly have been taken to the head of the queue. And there is no forum for discussing this sort of trauma and how to provide what is needed.

I moved away from the area but kept in touch as Susan's primary attachment figure. It did not seem right to break the relationship. A year or so later, I got a call from a social worker to say that Susan would have to move to residential care again, as she had exhausted all the support care workers in the town. He said that Susan could go anywhere in the country, so I opted for her to be placed near me. Again, it seemed the right thing to do. The care home really struggled and, during the 18 months she was there, Susan refused to get out of bed. To be got out of bed, I should say, as she could never do that herself. She did eat and put on weight, though. She would phone for a takeaway, showing an intellectual ability that did not fit with her emotional disability. This always confused the staff.

It was clear that Susan had to find somewhere else to live, so I set about finding a bungalow that would meet her needs. Once found, the ceiling tracking was added, the bathroom altered, and the kitchen made wheelchair-accessible. The doors were widened and a 'hospital' bed acquired. By this time, we had a care company and could provide some staff. But Susan was awarded direct payments with a management element included, so she began with these staff when she first moved. It very soon became apparent that the staff recruited were kind, well-meaning people, but had no experience of someone as strong-willed as Susan. From the beginning, she maintained control of the door entry system, only allowing in the people she wanted. Sometimes, this meant she would go hours without being able to use the toilet or get anything to eat, but her autonomy really mattered to her.

Eventually, it fell to our company to provide the care and support. And, with the necessary support for the staff to understand why Susan did what she did, we managed for some years. Later, the work was shared with another agency, as this gave Susan choice and the opportunity to reject one and for the other to take over.

Physically, Susan's condition was always going to be a cause for concern. She had physical health problems that required hospital stays from time to time. Susan's staff always spent time with her in hospital so as to help the nursing staff. This was always a strain but they managed. She developed a good relationship with the local taxi firm that had a wheelchair-accessible taxi. Susan was very competent with her electric wheelchair and could go most places she wanted to.

As Susan became more able to look outside of herself, she began to keep hamsters – albeit only one at a time and it was always very sad when they died. This was maintained for a while until the emotional strain of caring for a living creature when she had so little emotional strength herself became too much for her. Support staff found her quite a strain to be with much of the time, but they all felt privileged to support someone so strong-willed in such an unhelpful body. Susan never sought pity but she did seek understanding and had a strong sense of entitlement.

Susan's life expectancy was never going to be very long and she died quietly in her sleep at the age 51. I have lots of fond memories and learned a lot about how to support and care for people who are traumatised at or close to birth.

When I reflect on this particular piece of work, and the relationship I had with Susan, I can see that the model of understanding early trauma is not readily available to health and social care staff. The question must always be about whether this is too difficult for people to understand or just too painful for people to tolerate. I suspect it is the latter and this emphasises the need for the third element of the model, which is staff training and support. Many staff in social care received very little in the way of training and support and this needs to change.

The emphasis of this trauma-informed model is on unconscious processes, which traditionally were only ever addressed in psychoanalysis. The FAIT was always designed to capture the complexity of psychoanalytic understanding in a behavioural, observable way. Susan really demonstrates the impact of trauma on the development of self. I have met other people with severe cerebral palsy from birth experiences, and most of them have shown a similar difficulty in processing primary anger. It is perfectly normal and ordinary for helpless babies to be angry. The early emotional work for all of us is to develop the ability to live with those feelings and not act on the anger.

Melanie Klein referred to the resolution of the depressive position, which she described as the point at which a very young child becomes able to tolerate good and bad in the person caring for them. In moving from the practising stage to the rapprochement stage, we can see how that happens by observing the behaviour. This is more straightforward to understand than the deeper exploration of the unconscious.

There are never going to be enough resources to provide psychoanalysis for everybody. It is also unlikely that people with disabilities will receive that sort of therapeutic intervention. There are organisations such as Respond that provide individual therapy for people with disabilities and, within the Amara Care group of companies, we do provide individual therapy where it is indicated. But the beauty of the trauma-informed care model is that it can be made available to many more people, with good results. It is interesting to find that very often, when people are feeling much better, they cannot remember what it was that was bothering them in the first place. This is something we find with people who do not have disabilities, who attend for individual outpatient therapy. It does indicate that once the trauma is resolved, it is no longer there, and this can only be a good thing.

Susan did not resolve the trauma fully, but did come to an understanding of why she felt the way she did. She was able to talk about her family more openly and have some understanding of why her mother and sisters had struggled to cope with her. However, she could not ever accept that it was right. She did manage to grieve the loss of her father more, which was a good thing. Susan made it very clear before she passed away that she wanted to be buried locally to where she was living at the time and that she saw the company as her family. We did, of course, have an obligation to let her sisters know when she passed away and they did attend the funeral.

References

Klein, M. (1945) *Love, Guilt and Reparation*. London: Vintage.

Chapter 17:

Peace and Freedom – Dropping Everything to Pick up the Pieces

This title comes from what a number of people have now, after a life of turmoil and distress. The foundations of trauma and hopelessness are overcome eventually by the provision of the right support. And that can only come from a position of understanding and a willingness to change when change is needed.

The girl who kept dropping to the floor

Abigail suffers from epilepsy and has done so from a very young age. Witnessing seizures is hard for parents and family members, so experiencing seizures must be traumatic. The sudden and complete loss of control must be devastating. We cannot ever really imagine what that is like for the individuals concerned. Abigail does not have the words to tell us, either.

I remember the first time I was with someone when they experienced a grand mal seizure. It was very frightening for me and yet the other people present, who had seen it before, took it in their stride. This was in an old long-stay hospital for people with learning disabilities (known as 'mental handicap' or 'retardation' in those days) and quite a few people did have epilepsy. It was a good experience for me subsequently, as it showed me that people can recover from something that looks devastating.

It seemed like a novel idea when I suggested that the trauma behind Abigail's difficulties could be epilepsy. It is seen as a physical condition, treated with medication and generally quite well-controlled. It seemed a novel idea to think of the emotional impact of seizures – the biggest element, of course, being loss of control. Abigail had seizures from a young age and assessment of her emotional developmental stage revealed a lot of early behaviours. Some differentiation was shown with self-referenced behaviours such as a constant interest in her own appearance. There are lots of practising behaviours in repetitive speech and fixed patterns of using the environment. She has some early rapprochement behaviours and these are mostly showing as pseudo-seizures. It became clear that there was a complex relationship between the early trauma of seizures leaving her in a position of not being able to access her more able self. The pseudo-seizures were a response to feeling lost and helpless.

Unfortunately, for many years, the pseudo-seizures were treated as a challenging behaviour and responded to negatively. Abigail would fall to the floor, often at a very inconvenient time, and require help to get her up and functioning. Staff were irritated by the fact that they were not 'real' and would perhaps be negative and dismissive. If we frame the pseudo-seizures as a need for attention and reassurance, we can see that it is different, and the response needs to be different. If we meet the need for emotional security, the pseudo-seizures are not needed, and so they stop.

Once the understanding was reached, it was possible to look into ways of supporting Abigail that would accommodate the needs as well as help her to process the initial trauma. It required a holistic approach, taking into account the emotional disability in response to trauma as well as the learning disability elements that meant she would always need support. Abigail very much wanted to live alone and, at one stage, a single person service was arranged for her. But, as she had real seizures as well, it was not possible for her to have time alone and there was not sufficient funding for her to have staff 24 hours in a single person service.

The loss of the bungalow was a great blow to her and there was a period of more distress until she eventually settled into sharing with one other person in another bungalow in an ordinary street. The staff who support her are reliable and trained to provide the emotional support that a young child needs, with certainty about their presence and planned activities, and with no surprises. Abigail has thrived in this environment and pseudo-seizures are now rare. If they occur, they are seen as a reminder that the availability of a significant other – at all times – is a necessity, not a luxury.

The traumatic impact of epilepsy on early emotional development

The impact of early trauma is huge. It means that trauma on top of trauma is almost inevitable. Pre-verbal trauma cannot, by definition, be talked about. The individual does not have the words. Consequently, the response to later additional trauma can be confusing to the individual experiencing it and for those trying to help. If we reflect on what it is like for parents, we can see that trauma begets trauma, as all respond with fear. Imagine holding a small baby of a few months old that suddenly begins to have a seizure. Most of us have never seen this and the first response is likely to be panic. For the baby, who could not possibly understand, there must be real terror. And that is followed by hospital and examinations that, in themselves, are terrifying. This begins the pattern of trauma on top of trauma.

The element of loss of control is key. We never know when a seizure is going to happen. In time, the adults get used to it and start to respond practically, rather than in a panic. To the baby, then child and adult, it becomes a pattern in their life that they can do nothing about. Medication helps but it cannot always fully control. There are aspects of life that become less available, through us fearing that they will not cope.

The big question in terms of a holistic therapeutic approach is "Can it get better?". Can there be a way of supporting Abigail that allows for some processing of the trauma so as to reduce the response to distress? If we recognise and accept that the pseudo-seizures are a response to feelings of insecurity and fear, we can put in place support plans that reduce the risk of those feelings being activated. The consequence should be a reduction in pseudo-seizures. It may also be a reduction in real seizures, if they are triggered by anxiety and stress.

For Abigail, the medication worked quite well for the real seizures. There are times when the ambulance must be called and there may be an overnight stay in hospital. She is much more accepting now and can even enjoy the change of scenery and additional attention. The main thing is that Abigail can now say if she is feeling distressed, knowing she will get a warm and positive response without the increasing fear that would lead to a pseudo-seizure.

It has taken a lot of years to help people to understand the impact of early trauma. It has also been hard to gain acceptance of the confounding of trauma that follows. If we can accept that adults who have experienced serious trauma at the pre-verbal level can behave like a very young child when they are stressed, we can become more tolerant and accepting. There is no point in adopting an approach of "Pull yourself together!" when an individual clearly cannot. And, if the early trauma is not acknowledged, then there is repeated trauma on top. By the time we were able to offer the right approach, Abigail was desperately unhappy. She had few people in her life who mattered to her and was so misunderstood that her pseudo-seizures took on a 'cry for help' meaning. But the more pseudo-seizures Abigail had, the more irritated people were with her.

The question of cause and effect keeps coming up and it seems that facing a cause of early trauma before the age of one is extremely difficult, not to mention painful. We do not like to think of tiny dependent babies being traumatised. We need to think about premature babies who spend the first months of their lives in a neonatal intensive care unit. It is essential that they have the life-saving treatment or they would not be here at all. It is important, indeed vital, that the emotional impact is recognised and addressed. It is always better to intervene early and prevent secondary trauma, if at all possible.

The boy who kept dropping everything

Writing this reminds me of the little boy I reported on in 1992 (Frankish, 1992), who had a drop fit at 10 months. He was sitting on his mum's knee and fell to the floor, thereby experiencing trauma from the seizure and from the fall. I met him when he was five years old but, emotionally, he was still 10 months old; he dropped everything on the floor. Physically, he was fit and active but he was delayed intellectually (albeit not severely). He was very difficult to manage in school, as everything ended up on the floor.

Once we recognised the cause, we were able to put in place a therapeutic approach that included a named significant other at all times. There were teaching assistants at school, his mother at home, and a named key worker at respite care. He thrived and, within a year, he was moved to the top-class of the special school – with much older children – and was able to access his intellect. That was the beginning of the research that led to the FAIT.

I remember the initial response to the therapeutic intervention. I had asked the staff to carry him initially and they were wary, as he had previously had a habit of pinching their neck if he was picked up. But they agreed and he seemed to know that this was different. He reacted positively and within a couple of weeks he was willing to hold hands instead of being carried. A real success story.

The boy who kept dropping his trousers

If we go back to think about Abigail at the beginning of her story, we can reflect on how that particular behaviour developed and, similarly, in the little boy with the drop fits. It is extremely unlikely that anyone, at the time, would have associated the events that led to these behaviours as severely traumatic. This brings me back to the point I have made a number of times throughout this book – ie, trauma is idiosyncratic. What is traumatic for you may not be traumatic for me and vice versa. We do not know and cannot predict what anyone will find traumatic.

I remember the case of a young man who had an obsession with his bottom and that part of his anatomy. It became difficult for him to be out in public, as he would suddenly be touching himself or taking his trousers down. There was a fear that the behaviour was sexual and potentially dangerous. However, when I met him and talked with his family, it became clear that he was quite severely learning disabled and there was no indication of him wishing to interact with or hurt anyone. In fact, almost all his behaviours were self-referenced and all were at the differentiation stage of emotional development, indicating that his trauma was very early in life.

I asked his mother if she could remember anything that had happened in his early life – before the age of five – that had stuck with her or if she could recall an early event that had distressed him. She immediately responded by telling me of a time when they had been to the seaside and, driving back, he had screamed all the way home without them knowing what the matter with him was. When they got home and took off his nappy, they discovered that he had a huge reaction to something he'd eaten or drunk and his whole nappy area was raw.

Once we knew this, we could see what his present behaviour meant in terms of his trauma about that area of his body. It also meant that emotionally he was still about one year old and needed the emotional support of a child of that age. A programme of support was put in place to keep him connected and secure all of the time, so he never had to worry about having his needs met or being abandoned. We also talked to him about what had happened when he was a baby – although his comprehension was very limited so it was not possible to evaluate his understanding. We were, however, able to provide sufficient emotional security for him to be able to go out and about in contact with his significant other and without him having to go through any of his checking behaviours.

He had lived for many years with this distress without anyone understanding what it meant. As he was a young man with a fairly severe learning disability, it was assumed that his behaviour was because of his disability. This is something that we find all the time and it reminds me of the answer I used to get as a child when I asked why people behaved in a certain way: "It's because they're mentally handicapped." I know that that is not the right answer – as do many people now – but more people need to understand and be ready to accept the complexity of trauma. It should also be remembered that having a learning disability can in itself be traumatic, as it limits the understanding of what is happening, which in turn can lead to more fear.

A related issue is repeated trauma, which comes about when the initial trauma is not recognised or understood. The young man I just talked about was always in trouble and ostracised to some extent because people feared that there was something sexual about his behaviour. Every time he was rejected or left in a room by himself, he experienced further trauma with feelings of abandonment. This is very often the case when initial trauma is not recognised; then, the repeated trauma makes matters worse. Once the initial trauma has been recognised and the appropriate support package put in place, however, we do find that there is an immediate reduction in anxiety and then a gradual improvement in the emotional development stage.

The boy who kept dropping lit matches

I can think of so many trauma stories that I have heard over the years, including one young man who became a seriously dangerous firestarter. Following an exploration of his early life, we discovered that he had accidentally set fire to a litter bin as a very young child with a candle. We do not know if he was traumatised by the excitement of the fire or the reaction of the adults who discovered him, but he was clearly traumatised.

Sadly, he was compelled to repeat the initial experience, leaving him in a position of being held in a secure unit because his behaviour was so dangerous. His emotional difficulties could have been susceptible to positive outcome from treatment.

Very high-risk behaviour such as this will often lead to a detention order because of the danger to life. I do not argue against people being detained for safety reasons. However, I do argue that they should still receive therapeutic help to address their initial trauma and see if they are able to make decisions in the future that make them safe.

Looking for freedom, finding peace

The title of this chapter is peace and freedom so it might be worth exploring those concepts a little more in the light of the above-mentioned stories. Peace is something that we can all aspire to and wish for. When I visit distressed people for assessments or therapy, I am very conscious of the need for peace. Usually, by the time they get a referral to the psychology team, they have been living without peace for a long time and certainly without freedom.

The issue of freedom creates an awful lot of stress and distress in services. The DOLS (deprivation of liberty system) has put enormous strain on services and individuals. Although I can never accept that it is right to detain somebody who should not be detained, there does need to be some flexibility around providing safety without it feeling like detention.

I am aware of young women with multiple issues of disability and trauma putting themselves at risk by constantly walking into traffic or visiting areas of cities that are not safe. The process of asking the Court of Protection for permission to have a locked door is lengthy and sometimes difficult to argue. There does need to be a shared responsibility for decisions about locked doors for purposes of safety and proper record-keeping. I have always advocated that no one should be behind a locked door without someone standing at that door to maintain communication. I am aware that seclusion may not be used like this in hospital settings, but it is always better to maintain communication, as this helps the individual behind the locked door to understand that it is for their safety only.

Peace and freedom should be something that we can all experience in our daily lives. Sadly, this is not the case for so many people with trauma in their early lives. Clearly, the range of trauma is huge because – as I said before – it is idiosyncratic. The way we respond is the way we respond; we are all different. We will all react in a different way to life experiences. If we witness traumatic things when we are very small, it leaves a lasting image and impact on who we become.

References

Frankish, P. (1992) A psychodynamic approach to emotional difficulties within a social framework. *Journal of Intellectual Disability Research* 36: 559–563

Chapter 18:
Support and Trust

Carrie Anne Smith

Carrie Anne has Dissociative Identity Disorder (DID). This means that there are multiple personalities in the same body, of both genders, all ages and including some animals. Carrie Anne's pronouns are non-gender specific.

The Diagnostic and Statistical Manual of Mental Disorders (Fifth Edition) (DSM-5) states that, for a person to meet the diagnostic criteria for Dissociative Identity Disorder (DID), at least two enduring personalities must be present – each with their own enduring pattern of thinking and perceiving the world. By way of example, a male alter (alternate personality or identity) in a female body may choose to wear masculine clothes rather than a dress. It was all so confusing and, prior to coming into the support of Amara Care, this is where we found ourselves after many years of being misunderstood, mental health misdiagnoses, and losing time.

When we arrived at Amara Care, we well and truly landed with a big, confused bump! We had a new and official diagnosis of DID (Frankish and Sinason, 2017) and Complex Post-Traumatic Stress Disorder (CPTSD), which is characterised by recurrent and intrusive bad memories, flashbacks, nightmares, and relational difficulties. We had also just come from a very unsafe and ritually abusive situation, in which we were regularly being abused, as the perpetrators had known where we lived. Ritual abuse occurred with a Satanic ideology in our case and it incorporates physical, sexual, ideological, mental and emotional abuse alongside ritual abuse itself. With this in mind, and with the help of Dr Pat Frankish, we were moved into the care of Amara Care to begin our new lives.

When we got there, we were given a dedicated team of support staff, who looked after us 24/7 and even did overnight sleeps with us. This was something that we could not get our thinking around because we were not aware, nor did we believe, that people could think that we mattered enough to be given all this support when really we were just a little set of mind-control slaves. Nevertheless, however, these people wanted to know us – even the dark parts of us – and just accepted us for who we are. This was to be a new start for us, with real therapeutic relationships and a group of support workers who really seemed to care about us.

We will never forget waking up on that first morning after we got here. The sun was shining, the birds were singing and all was peaceful, which was something that we were far from used to – coming from a town that was anything, for us, but safe. Everything was so different to what we were used to and, when we went through to the kitchen from our bedroom, our support staff member was there with a cheerful smile and a kind word; nothing was too much trouble. We felt like taking a long relaxing breath because finally we were safe and, unbeknown to us, our lives would never be the same again.

Over the proceeding weeks, some of our alters from our DID system came to visit the staff, and Elaine (who was in charge of our service) accepted every one of them. Even our dark alters, who could be viewed as 'bad' and ritual-loyal alters, were accepted – except for when they did something that was not OK, when they were then challenged and told to try taking some time out until they could be nice! The fact of the matter was that Elaine, and our whole staff team, were there to keep us safe. Some of the dark and distressed alters in our system were prone to self-harm and suicidal tendencies because of their mind control and ritualistic past (Frankish and Smith, 2022), so they also needed keeping safe from themselves.

With all this wonderful support came in-depth psychology sessions from Dr Pat Frankish and these would prove to be vital in our moving on. We now believe that all living beings have the capacity to heal, change and grow; looking back on those days when we first came, we were far from being in this place. However, this was still a pivotal moment in our road to beginning to heal. This seemed to be quite a peaceful period in our lives, with alters trying out new things with their support staff that they had never done before, and our safe base to live came with a newfound security that we had never felt in our lives until then. However, after a couple of months, our darker alters made a move to make their mark, which was a sign that the honeymoon period was well and truly over!

Pat, our psychologist, already knew that we had suicidal mind control and other complex and experimental programming (Frankish and Smith, 2022). She understood that this was something that we needed to be kept safe from and, as such, we lived with this hanging over our heads a little like the sword of Damocles. It scared most of us; however, our staff and Pat were very strong-willed and kept on challenging the attempts by the dark alters to bring this mind control to fruition, much to their complete distaste. It was what was needed then and remains the case today, because this is something that we still live with.

The staff soon learned how to watch out for the negative behaviour that these alters exhibited and, thanks to weekly staff support meetings with Pat, the staff's knowledge of how to work with us grew and grew. The dark alters were not particularly pleased with regard to these meetings – although they turned out to be the best thing that our staff could have had, as it gave them knowledge in the fight against the dark ones.

Meet the hosts

We have no core personality in our DID system, which means our youngest alter is just a baby who speaks by communicating a 'ma ma ma' noise. When we first came to where we now live, Sara was the host of our collective, and this continued for some time. After a while, however, this changed to deaf and non-verbal alters hosting; this brought with it a set of whole new ways of working with us, which our staff soon adapted to.

Jennifer and Firefly, the non-verbal alters

The staff soon learned that, because they did not know how to do British Sign Language (BSL), they could not communicate with Jennifer, who is deaf and the next host. So, the staff adapted to this situation by having Jennifer write to them, and then writing back to her. This may have been long-winded but it had the effect of making Jennifer much more at ease and she was able to communicate with others in this way for the first time ever. This gave Jennifer the confidence to 'talk' to staff and soon she was building therapeutic relationships with them.

Next came Firefly, who was non-verbal but could speak in BSL. This alter had a very strange view of the world and the people in it. As such, she could not properly connect with people, and many of her attachments to staff members were misunderstood by them.

Firefly thought that she could communicate with people through the power of thought and the human mind and even sat in her wheelchair in a busy bus station, giving the people there a dressing-down (through the power of thought alone) on how to understand her. Of course, she was soon distressed because no one actually *could* understand her. Firefly signified a very difficult time for our support staff but, through the support of Pat and a lot of teamwork, they managed to get through this period together.

Charisma and Cathartic, trust and rest

The next hosts were our twins Charisma and Cathartic, who are ten years old. These two girls were named thus because their abusers told them that the twins should have 'charisma' when doing their job (which was to do forensic clean-ups after acts of heinous abuse of victims by the abusers), because it would be 'cathartic' for them to do so.

They had never known fun times and this was something that Amara Care's support staff team soon identified, allowing the twins to have more fun in an effort to undo the learned behaviour that the bad people had taught them. Charisma and Cathartic came to know laughter and funny times, as well as cookery lessons from Elaine, and were taught to live life as the ten-year-olds that they were – all thanks to the staff who were working with them.

Around this time, our support staff team were becoming drained and tired from having to work with our trauma and dark alters all the time, and so they decided to increase their team size to around 15 staff members (some of whom were male) in short shifts. This overwhelmed our whole DID system, as we could not get used to having males within our group, and – coupled with many staff that we did not know – this became too much. After a short while, however, the trust between Pat and ourselves saw the restoration of our original staff team, who were refreshed and were able to continue their work with us.

I include this to show that – although the staff team was enlarged – Pat and her team soon realised that trust is a fragile thing, especially with so many people involved. They ended up doing the best for their staff and the best for us and I will ever be grateful to them for this. Back then, we did not fully understand this; however, now we know that everybody needs a break, especially when working with trauma. Pat and her team allowed everyone to take gentle care of themselves while continuing to protect a system (with complex behaviour) at the same time.

Jenevieve

During this time, Jenevieve made an appearance and really confused our support staff team because she was unable to move or talk and was only able to communicate by using one blink for 'yes' and two blinks for 'no'. Jenevieve was hard on our staff team, as she usually emerged when we were laid on the sofa or our bed, but it was very evident to the team that Jenevieve had suffered a LOT of trauma – some of which remains a mystery even today.

We continue to work with her as and when she comes into the body, though, and she holds a special place in our heart. We have since discovered that Jenevieve was traumatised when she was trying to get away from her coven attackers.

Alistair

Alistair also arrived on the scene not long after we found that we were safe. He is a hot-headed male, who can finally laugh and tell silly jokes after years of trauma and can be great fun if he trusts people. This was not always where Alistair was at, though. For a long time, Alistair held a lot of trauma and not one of our DID system really knew why or, indeed, what had happened to him. Also, because there are so many alters in our system, any host who may have followed on from Alistair (as it were) would be so fragmented that it would not be possible for them to follow his narrative.

Alistair eventually disclosed his trauma to Dr Pat Frankish in psychology sessions. He had been subjected to the traumas of murder and – to name but a few – and, as such, was very traumatised indeed. Pat kept his confidence and encouraged him to begin to believe that what happened was not his fault (because it wasn't), but he sure felt responsible for things that had happened. He still feels guilty every now and then, but we try to make him feel reassured in the knowledge that he is heard and seen and that it is not his fault.

As Alistair began to heal, we discovered that he actually had a wicked sense of humour. On one occasion, his support staff came in to find that Alistair had come into the body, and he was dressed in a rather girly-style attire. Realising this, Alistair looked at his staff member and said: "I'm dressed in pink!" With a complete look of disgust on his face, Alistair looked in our wardrobe for a more masculine attire. He was soon wearing his favourite football top and feeling much happier and more comfortable – much to the distaste of the girls that reside within our system!

Meet the system

Since then, there have been many hosts, some of whom have been around for a while and others for only a short time. All this time, however, alters have been working in therapy with Dr Pat Frankish. In our system, there are 2,643 fragmented and 'full' alters, many subsystems within our main system, and animal, female and male alters – all co-existing within one body – and a number of them have found that they have a voice in therapy.

To begin with, a lot of mind control information came out in these sessions, but Pat took all of this information in her stride. Little children and teenagers all came out and soon it was discovered how complex we actually all are as a system. Indeed, Dr Valerie Sinason (Frankish and Sinason, 2017) – who helped us to have our first encounter with Pat – said that we are one of the most complex DID collectives in the country.

Pat worked with us for some time and, when she retired, she handed us over to Dr Natalie Cross and latterly Sue Walker, with whom we still work today. Thanks to us feeling safer in the here and now and having a safe place to live, alters who are dark have now been coming forward and giving more detailed facts about what happened to us. We have alters who can draw maps of where acts of abuse, etc, occurred. This has all been possible because of a safe base, dedicated staff team, and psychology sessions, which are part of Dr Pat Frankish's model for the support of people with complex needs.

Meet Carrie-Anne

I, Carrie-Anne, have been the longest host to our system. I came along at a very dark time for our DID system and have got us through a lot! I come with my own set of trauma, and I don't always get it right, but I am getting there. When the NHS and social services decided that we no longer needed 24/7 support, despite our complex needs, Amara Care did everything they could to help us. Through the support of Amanda Brock and Dr Pat Frankish, we fought these two bodies and – although we got nowhere with our efforts – we are still fighting to live a meaningful life every day, which is Amara Care's motto. To be precise, its motto is 'Supporting Meaningful Lives', and this is exactly what their staff have done. To be honest as well, our lives are owed to Pat and Amanda, as they rescued us when we were acutely unwell and needed to be kept safe. We will never be able to thank them enough.

Back to life with DID, however. As a host of our system, I work with our support staff to achieve the activities of daily living and blend this with doing things that are fun and meaningful, so that we have a richer life. Staff accompany us to medical appointments in case another alter comes out and they need help to understand what is being said. Staff also help us to go shopping and provide us with companionship, which is something that is very important to us. If we did not have the companionship of our support staff, then we could have become isolated and very lonely indeed, as many people in society today do not understand DID very well (or CPTSD, for that matter). This is something that we are grateful for because, without our staff, we would not be able to live our lives in such a positive manner.

Bringing dark alters to light

Now we are trying in therapy to deal with the dark alters that are left in this DID system. Bearing in mind that we have been working in therapy with Pat and her colleagues for more than 15 years, it may seem to the reader that it is impossible to 'cure' dark alters of their mind control and ritualistic behaviours, but this is simply not true.

After all these years of therapy, we are still encountering very dark alters, such as the hypnotiser and Nemesis. Yet even the hypnotiser is slowly starting to talk to our psychologist Sue Walker and bring to the table facts that would prove our abuse, so there is hope for justice if he becomes ready and able to do so. The dark alters have seen grave atrocities and thus need to heal, but some of them are not there yet. So we keep working with them, the protectors in our system keep trying to rally around the darker ones, and we hope to one day be able to help them heal, change and grow.

Seeing the light with clients

Another fundamental aspect of our healing has been being on the journey with people with learning disabilities and their support staff. The clients that are a part of Amara Care have taught us a lot about simplicity and that long words do not need to be brought into the equation – rather, just by saying things how they are but in a very gentle way, you will get more done.

The clients have brought laughter to our lives when we have been depressed, brought calm when there has been nothing but anger, and created beautiful friendships when we have not had any. These people have taught these university undergraduates so very much and more about emotional intelligence than many other human beings that I have met. They are pure gold and I will always be grateful to them!

From host to co-ordinator

As time moved on, as previously mentioned, we lost our 24/7 support. Although we battled to keep it, the NHS decided that it was not enough to have DID and complex needs because the professionals we saw did not really seem to understand our condition. We were beside ourselves at this point and, after Amanda and Pat had supported us themselves, we had to lose four of our overnight sleeps a week simply because social services had – in our opinion – little knowledge of how to help people with DID and dropped the overnight sleeps like a hot potato. Perhaps in time this may be reversed because we do not sleep, owing to our not feeling safe at all, and now we are under a new government. However, Amara Care were to give us an offer that we really were not expecting.

On the journey down to Rowan House one morning, I heard Amanda Brock say to me: "I am giving you a job offer."

"Pardon?" I said, and stopped wheeling my wheelchair.

"I want to see if you can manage with the responsibility of a job first," Amanda continued. "So, if you volunteer for a while, we will then be able to see if you can manage to do this."

I felt shock as she then asked me to create a timetable for activities groups to lead people with learning disabilities into, as she believed that I would make a good activities co-ordinator for them. At the time of writing, three years ago tomorrow (to the day!), I was accepted – with a part-time contract, following a full DBS check and job interview – into the role of an activities co-ordinator for Amara Care.

I have worked with groups providing group support for people with learning disabilities – groups that teach them life skills such as cookery and manners, along with more fun skills such as music, drama and arts and crafts (to name but a few). I am also now able to provide one-to-one work with different clients in a variety of subjects. We do this because we have been in the client's shoes ourselves, have walked their path with them, and now are trailblazers that can honestly say: "If I can aim for the moon, then so can you!" I love my job and it is a privilege to work with these individuals.

I feel that our DID helps us to do this role, because different alters in our system have knowledge of a plethora of different subjects, with which we can teach our clients. Some of our alters are creative in that they can write poetry and some were born to teach numeracy and literacy, whereas others can teach performing arts and get all of our clients laughing. I am then given knowledge of these different subjects from them and this helps me to do my job to the best of my ability.

I have also been given the opportunity to become qualified with a Level 3 award in education and training, which qualifies me to teach adult education, and this is all down to Amanda and Pat's belief in us and our abilities. I also qualified with a Level 2 in counselling skills, which helps in my role of running a small friendship talking group once a week. Were it not for Pat and Amanda, we would most likely have no life, yet now we have a meaningful life.

We were taken from a place where – chances are – we would have ended up dead, and were gently placed in the home that we never even knew we needed, and have been provided with the ongoing support that we never even believed that we deserved. Amara Care has become more than a job and its staff have become more than just supporters or friends; they have turned into the family that we never really, had. These people are our heroes. And, even though we still need support and may always need it, we are getting there slowly but surely.

What is evident from our encounters with all Amara Care support and psychology staff is that trust has been gained by the staff, who have worked so tirelessly to make us safe. To an abuse survivor, trust is very fragile, so – if anyone is able to gain the trust of that abuse survivor – then they know they are on the correct track. Most of our staff have gained our fragile trust, and we always tell them that they are honoured to gain this, and most of them know this deep in their own hearts.

Life is very different in many ways now. Where once we were a breeder (which is a collection of alters who breed children at the coven's command) and had children for the coven to abuse and sacrifice, now we are having the chance to properly grieve them and acknowledge our losses, and – while we still miss them like crazy – we know they are in the loving arms of God.

Where once we did not have a safe base, we now own our own home. This came about because one of our abusers (the father) died intestate and Amara Care facilitated us buying our own home.

Finally, where once we were abused and tortured, now we have peace and most of all a modicum of hope – a lasting and enduring hope that one day we may find a true sense of justice. The road to healing may be a long one but, boy, it is a path worth treading.

Thank you, Dr Pat Frankish and Amanda Brock and all the staff within Amara Care Ltd. You have shown us a new and safe pathway that we will never forget. We thought we would be dead by age 40, but you saved us. For that, we will be forever grateful and will never forget any of you!

Amara Saves

Amara Care is a place of peace
A place to find real release
For within its staff is safety's place
A place to shine out, full of grace
I know not why they took me in that day
But with them, I have found my way
I know I still have struggle's path

But it is a way out of the aftermath.
Amara do all that they can
Since my journey first began
To save people from trauma's path

Until you reach a place to laugh
Amara to me does mean 'saves'
To help me in all they gave
And give of themselves every day
Until your cares start to go away.

If I could give Amara one big wish
It would be to give a dish
Full of 'thank you's from the heart
For all the saving that you start
And follow through and keep doing so
Until you feel a bright warm glow
However you feel, they want to help
'Amara Saves', really can be felt.

So, when you feel down and out
There is no need to scream and shout
For even though I've far to go
Even I can work and show
That Amara Saves, and carries on
Where others have dread and away have gone
Amara cares – and saves – is there
When no one else does seem to care.

References

Frankish, P. and Sinason, V. (2017) *Holistic Therapy for People with Dissociative Identity Disorder*. London: Karnac.

Frankish, P. and Smith, C.A. (2022) *Trauma and Dissociation*. Shoreham: Pavilion Publishing.

Chapter 19:
Future Possibilities

If we reflect on the material in this book, we come to an understanding of the need to both recognise and respond to early traumatic experiences. This leads to asking: "What do we do about it?"

One aim must be to try and reduce the amount of trauma that is experienced, by providing information and support to all new parents and all neonatal care staff, as well as early years staff in all types of facilities. We must always remember that trauma and the response to trauma is idiosyncratic. We all react in our own way, so being fully person-centred is essential.

It is not as easy as recognising spots as chicken pox or coughs as chest infections. The subtlety of the change in perception of the world after trauma is recognisable, but we need to be alert to it. Lots of parents have described to me the day that their child changed, but they did know what it meant or what to do, or even that they could do anything.

Trauma-informed neonatal care

It is extremely difficult for the impact of trauma on babies in neonatal intensive care units to be recognised. Their fragile life, and the physical support to maintain life, must take priority. It is hard to think about the impact of putting needles into a tiny baby. Parents and care staff have to cope with their own feelings as well. Providing emotional support for all is not only desirable; it is essential if all are to thrive.

We have been able to describe therapeutic interventions that help, but prevention would be ideal. Awareness and skills training for all neonatal staff would be hugely helpful. The stage of emotional development would be symbiosis – ie, the stage we rarely see in later referrals. This does not mean that symbiosis does not exist after the first few weeks of life but, rather, that people who are so cut off from others are often seen as not able to communicate and respond. They are rarely recognised as locked down by trauma. Encouraging skin-to-skin contact is very positive for the symbiotic stage.

Establishing a symbiotic relationship with a shutdown baby or child is possible but not easy. It is similar to the establishment of a therapeutic relationship with anyone and requires constant positive regard (with no demands), contact in a safe warm reliable relationship, and lots of patience. Providing positive regard eventually leads to the recipient noticing. This can be very subtle at first and can be a glance, a relaxation of tense muscles, or maybe a smile. Once it happens, there is something to build on – gently and quietly – until there is a meaningful connection. It is challenging work but has its rewards.

When we find an older child or adult who has shut down and is cut off from everyone, we could instigate a 'contact programme'. This involves approaching the person at planned regular intervals (eg, every 30 minutes) and smiling, speaking and maybe touching gently. If this is put in place, within a few days or weeks, the individual will look up when you approach. Once that happens, contact can be built on and emotional development will occur. It has not been straightforward, but I have managed to make this work a few times. Sadly, half doing it can make matters worse, as it confirms to the shutdown person that there is nothing better. Investing in appropriate care and support at the beginning of life for traumatised babies should have a significant impact on their development and reduce the level of distress we see in children who have had a traumatic start in life.

Giving all staff in neonatal and early years provision the knowledge and training in how to notice and alleviate the consequences of trauma would be well worth doing and ultimately save a lot of distress later. The financial savings would also be considerable, as the need for expensive secure facilities and such like would be reduced. We have never been very good at preventing mental ill-health. If only there was a vaccine, we may achieve more. But the vaccine is human contact and that, alas, is very variable in availability and skill.

A trauma-informed approach to neurodiversity

Moving on from the early years, we can look at school-age children and consider the huge increase in SEND referrals during the past few years. There has been a huge increase in concerns about the incidence of autism and ADHD, along with a range of neurodivergence. It may be that there are lots of reasons behind this and there might be a discovery of something biological. In the absence of this information, we can look at the presentation as an aspect of emotional development. If more information becomes available, leading to another approach to treatment, then we can follow what that might be.

In the interim, it is worth considering this model of emotional development. We may not be able to identify a triggering trauma, but we can recognise the presentation and consider interventions that may help. We do not know how fixed the brain becomes so we do not know if there is anything that can change the fundamental functioning. We can, however, look at ways of helping the emotional development towards individuation and self-sufficiency.

One of the key features of emotional maturation to individuation is the ability to consider someone else and their thoughts and needs. Neurodivergent people are usually more self-referenced and unable to predict the thoughts and feelings of others. Aiding the development of rapprochement behaviours can be a positive way forward. It would mean working on the principle that something potentially traumatic underpins the difficulty in relating, but this may never be identified specifically.

It does seem helpful, however, to observe the individual and assess the behaviour in terms of emotional developmental stage. If this observation shows arrested emotional development at the practising/early rapprochement cusp (found most frequently), then care and support plans can be put in place to aid further development. With children of average or above average intelligence, the work can be about enabling thoughts to become the prime movers. They can learn to make choices after evaluating specific instances instead of just reacting.

One example would be the known tendency for autistic children to say whatever comes into mind, with no consideration of the impact on others. As a practising behaviour, they are doing what they can. If they are provided with an emotionally nurturing and supportive intervention, they can learn to choose not to speak without thinking. It does not necessarily alter the primary neurodivergent condition, but it helps with communication and potentially produces more positive relationships.

Within a classroom this would require providing the neurodivergent child or children with certainty about where their emotional security rests, who they turn to if they need help, and specific plans for each individual. One-to-one support is often provided for these children, so it is about clarifying that the role of the one-to-one person includes elements of emotional development as well as academic learning.

Throughout my career, I have been involved with lots of cases of the same nature as those described above. Sometimes the support is in tune with the need and all goes well. Unfortunately, sometimes resources are not sufficient and the one-to-one support becomes shared between too many people. It would be good if all SEND plans included appropriate guidance on this issue. I can reflect on some excellent interventions that have resulted in young people successfully going on to senior school with enough personal and social skills to accommodate their own difference, as well as the tolerance of others' non-understanding.

Applying the trauma-informed model of care in secondary schools

Let's move on now to senior school children and the pain of puberty. Young people who are not fully individuated react badly to the movement to other rooms and classes that comes with secondary school. The safety and certainty of the classroom and teacher is lost. This may be the first time that the emotional disability is noticed, because it has not been challenged before. With the stress and anxiety that is provoked, there may be a deterioration in behaviour, leading to detention and exclusion. The child who is already feeling lost and out of step will possibly feel safer in the internal exclusion room with one member of staff and the certainty of what happens next. It can become a perverse incentive.

If delayed emotional development is noted, it is possible to put in place the necessary settings to manage and promote development. This would involve making sure that the child is welcomed by name into the classroom and directed to where to sit, with an explanation of what happens next. Problem-solving exercises can be added in form time at the beginning of the day. Starting these simple adjustments early can usually prevent escalation to more problems and eventual exclusion.

Having observed many children in classrooms I can identify the lost children. But there is an opportunity to intervene between the ages of 11 and 16, which is preferable to letting things deteriorate to the next age period. I am aware that teachers want to teach, rather than be therapists or care staff. But there are so many young people who do not have a strong enough sense of self that it needs to be addressed. Enabling a child to find their place in the world before they leave school must surely be worthwhile.

There is a need to recognise and accept the increase in neurodiversity, increase in multi-parent homes, and the impact of social media and rapid communication. If a young person trusts the information on their phone more than their teachers or parents, they are showing that their significant other is their phone. As a reliable attachment figure, the phone is not reliable or real. It is a further sign of the changes in modern life that are mitigating against secure self-knowledge and increasing the incidence of fragile mental health. There is plenty of evidence of this issue but little in terms of a coherent understanding and response.

If we consider the young person who is still struggling with infantile development of self when they hit puberty, and the work of establishing an adult self, we can see how the issues compound. There are a huge number of young people, in their teens and early 20s, who are directionless and struggling to find a place in the world. They are vulnerable to exploitation by any 'leader' who offers the certainty of a place to belong and a set of rules to follow. We see this in the drug and gambling cartels that are now commonplace. Our failure to help young people earlier leaves them vulnerable to negative influences. Drug-taking can become an escape and, tragically, often leads to death. It would be helpful if there was a shared understanding of the factors that predict the problem and if they could be addressed in a preventative way.

Transforming support services

Modern mental healthcare has become overwhelmed and less effective. As the pressure of numbers has increased, the quality and depth of response has decreased. We hear on the news daily that people have been failed by mental health services. It has become the norm for people in distress to be offered short-term interventions or to wait months to see anyone. In the meantime, the individual remains lost and un-anchored. The absence of a secure emotional base is critical.

For people with an additional intellectual disability, all the foregoing can be worse or better. Many people with intellectual disabilities will have a support package of some sort, which can be helpful and effective because it provides the secure emotional base that is needed. However, some will be even worse off than those with average intelligence, because they may end up escalating through the system to secure detention. They may have the benefit of acceptance that they have a right to receive care, which is not necessarily there for the mainstream mental health group, but they may have less influence on where they get support. If they manage to secure a referral to supported living with a trauma-informed care model, they have the opportunity to do well. Early trauma and interference in the development of self will be addressed and real growth of personality will happen.

Hopefully, a future Mental Health Act will provide a framework for some of these things to happen. It needs to link fully with health and social care procedures so as to stop the buck passing from one service to the other. A holistic approach, which is person-centred and recognises the existence and significance of a defined self, is vital to the well-being of everyone. The Mental Capacity Act needs to accommodate these trauma needs, too. There is a need to recognise the difference between emotional disability and intellectual disability. Clearly, some people will have both, but we need to recognise that people can have an emotional disability that presents more as a mental health issue. This group is over-represented in prisons, homeless people, and revolving-door mental health services. We do know much more now than we used to about the impact of trauma, and this must be taken into account when looking at new services.

We have shown that it is possible to help and to prevent problems arising. This collection of stories, and the underpinning story of Amara Care, demonstrate the effectiveness of the person-centred humanistic approach to distress that understands distress as a response to traumatic events in early childhood. It is painful to think about babies and toddlers being traumatised. It is perhaps easier to see how it happens to children with learning disabilities. But it can happen to any of us and the impact is significant. The way to ameliorate it is clear and simple but requires a complete shift in the way help is provided. The institutions were a response to not knowing what to do with lots of distressed people who had no work, no money, no proper housing and no health service. The NHS was a further response to the same problems. It is now time to address the core issues with a unified message that all children are valued.

Furthermore, there is a need to recognise and accept that issues missed in early childhood will become major issues later. The foundations of the holistic model of trauma-informed care came from John Bowlby and Donald Winnicott in the 1960s and 1970s. We need to learn from them and build on the knowledge we now have of a way of working that captures the essence of people and all they have to offer.

The application of the stage model of emotional development described by Mahler has given us the FAIT and a simple method for identifying the emotional developmental stage. Using this in all support services would make a huge difference to the individuals concerned. As there is more acknowledgement of individual needs through initiatives such as the Oliver McGowan Mandatory Training on Learning Disability and Autism, we can be hopeful that change is coming.

A final call to action

As I sit writing this, I hear a report on the radio about people with intellectual disabilities who are kept in segregation (evidently, 2,000 people in the UK). It is time their trauma was properly recognised and the re-traumatising stopped. There was a significant piece of work done a few years ago to carry out some independent reviews of people who were detained and kept in isolation. I was involved in carrying out some of those reviews and was distressed by what I found in some facilities – although, to be fair, most people were trying to do their best for the people they were caring for. The difficulty was that they had no accurate formulation on which to base their care plans.

There is still a tendency to look for behavioural approaches to challenging behaviour without recognising that the challenging behaviour should be described as distressed behaviour in the first instance and that the treatment approach should then be planned around the relief of distress. Once we acknowledge that the distress is present, we can begin to look at ways to help. One of the things that has become clear to me during the past few years is that, once people have understood the impact of trauma on individual development, they can empathise and work kindly with very distressed people. We need to get to the point of recognising distress and accept that the way forward must be kind, tolerant and therapeutic.

We have tried, throughout this volume, to put the present position in a historical context and to put forward ways of working that we know can work. A lot of this is charted in my history over the past 40 years and in the learning that has come from starting in the old institutions and progressing to supported living within a trauma-informed model. It seems to me that it is possible to provide the right care for the right people at the right time, if only we have the will to make it happen. I see the potential for a better future for the very vulnerable people that have been addressed throughout these stories. I recognise my colleagues and the people working in relevant services for their contribution to our understanding of the need to recognise and respond to early traumatic experiences. I call upon all those in positions of power, as well as all holders of resources, to invest in a trauma-informed model for the future.

It is hard to think about how long this message has been articulated and made available to us. This does raise the question of what the cause of the inability to hear or see what needs to be done is. John Bowlby and Donald Winnicott were very clear in their message to society and the powers that be. The question concerns why they could not be heard and why it is so difficult to be heard nowadays. We have found, in Amara Care and our group of companies, that sometimes people can recognise the need and provide the appropriate support for the needs to be met. It is not impossible and certainly is replicable. It does, however, require a rethink on the way that services are commissioned for the complex people whose trauma is missed in the early stages.

The system for planning services and funding them seems too constrained to allow for proper provision to complex people. We can only hope that some of those people who are in positions of power will do something about it. I was consulted more than a year ago by a representative from NHS England to propose a way forward. At the time, I felt optimistic that something would happen, but sadly I have heard nothing further. As with the discussions with Doncaster College about the possibility of a master's-level course in disability psychotherapy, it will almost certainly be a lack of funding that will prevent anything happening.

And yet the system is wasting money by spending huge sums on inappropriate packages of interventions that potentially leave people in isolation for many years. I reflect on the scandal that led to the closure of the big hospitals because of the treatment that the people inside were receiving. I reflect on recent exposures of systemic failures, such as the abuse and neglect at Winterbourne View private hospital, and I know that there are inappropriate services across our country (and across the world). I know it is not easy if you are running a large service and you have only one or two very complicated people. But there is no doubt that if you address the few complicated people appropriately, it takes the pressure off everybody else.

I hope, if you have read this book from the beginning, that you found stories that will encourage you to take forward the ideas and the model. The model of trauma-informed care is based on sound theoretical studies of human behaviour, unconscious material, and therapeutic approaches that work. It is certainly no more expensive to do it properly than it is to provide locked units and revolving-door situations.

I am coming to the end of my working life and this may be, I think, my last publication. I rely on all those who are reading this book to take the work forward for the benefit of all, because it is not just the people with the complex needs that suffer – it is their relatives, the staff supporting them, and the whole of society. Trauma is not confined to the few; it is there for all of us. But those who are multiply disadvantaged by trauma and other conditions need our attention and help urgently.

References

Bowlby, J. (1988) *A Secure Base: Clinical Applications of Attachment Theory*. London; Routledge.

Winnicott, D.W. (1990) *Home Is Where We Start From*. Middlesex; Penguin.

Poem

When you start out with Amara Care
Very quickly you know that they're going to be there
From a negative past and trauma too
You find they encompass all of you
Positivity and warmth do abound
And warm voices that make this a very clear sound
You start to know people that you can trust
And knowing you can have a hug is a must.

If you're not used to positive attachments you will find
This is the place to leave all that behind
A safe place to live and a dedicated team
To look after you if you know what I mean
Safe psychological support is there when you need
And everything's there for you, yes indeed
A lovely safe time you can have with some fun
Your new life with Amara has just begun.

So never despair when you're in your staff's support
We triumph with you as you progress as cohorts
All bound together with one purpose, one aim
You start to feel better and never the same
A meaningful life from the very start
All of these things will warm your very heart
and from there you'll never feel alone
Because you have allies so you're not on your own.